Nikon Z8

Beginner's Guide

A Comprehensive Guide to Capturing and Editing Images & Videos with the Nikon Z8 Camera

Elior Weston

Copyright © 2024 **Elior Weston**

All Rights Reserved

This book or parts thereof may not be reproduced in any form, stored in any retrieval system, or transmitted in any form by any means—electronic, mechanical, photocopy, recording, or otherwise—without prior written permission of the publisher, except as provided by United States of America copyright law and fair use.

Disclaimer and Terms of Use

The author and publisher of this book and the accompanying materials have used their best efforts in preparing this book. The author and publisher make no representation or warranties with respect to the accuracy, applicability, fitness, or completeness of the contents of this book. The information contained in this book is strictly for informational purposes. Therefore, if you wish to apply the ideas contained in this book, you are taking full responsibility for your actions.

Printed in the United States of America

TABLE OF CONTENTS

TABLE OF CONTENTS III

CHAPTER ONE 1

INTRODUCTION 1

CHAPTER TWO 9

GETTING STARTED WITH YOUR CAMERA 9

    IMPORTANT BUTTONS AND CONTROLS FOR THE CAMERA INITIAL SETUP 9
    NAVIGATING THE TOUCHSCREEN 11
    LANGUAGE SELECTION 13
    CONFIGURING TIME ZONE AND DATE 14
    POWERING UP: BATTERY INSTALLATION AND CHARGING 16
    ATTACHING THE LENS 17
    ADJUSTING DIOPTER SETTINGS 19
    INSTALLING A MEMORY CARD 20

CHAPTER THREE 22

GOING OVER THE CAMERA EXTERNAL BUTTONS AND CONTROLS ... 22

    TOP SIDE CONTROLS AND FEATURES 22
    BACK VIEW CONTROLS AND FEATURES 24
    FRONT VIEW CONTROLS AND FEATURES 26

CHAPTER FOUR: HOW TO USE THE CAMERA METERING MODES 29

    SELECTING THE RIGHT METERING METHOD 30
    EXPLORING THE VARIOUS METERING TYPES 31
        Matrix Metering *31*
        Center-weighted Metering *33*
        Spot Metering Mode *34*
        Highlight-weighted Metering *35*
    MANAGING NOISE IN METERING 37

CHAPTER FIVE 39

HARNESSING THE POWER OF HDR 39

    AUTOMATIC HDR FUNCTIONALITY 40
    UTILIZING BRACKETING AND MERGE TO HDR FOR IMAGING 43

CHAPTER SIX 46
UTILIZING Z8 BRACKETING FEATURES 46

How to use the White Balance Bracketing 47
How to use the ADL Bracketing 49

CHAPTER SEVEN 52
THE FLASH 52

Electronic Flash 52
Selecting a Flash Synch Mode 54
Ghost Images 56
Handling Sync Speed Issues 57
High-Speed Sync 58
How to Use External Flash 60
How to Use Flash Exposure Compensation 62

CHAPTER EIGHT 64
UNDERSTANDING AND USING THE EXPOSURE MODES ON THE Z8 .. 64

Mastering F-stops and Shutter Speeds 65
Achieving Equivalent Exposure 67
Calculating Exposure Correctly 68
Analyzing the Various Exposure Types 69
  Aperture Priority (A) 69
  Shutter Priority (S) 70
  Program Mode (P) 70
  Manual Mode (M) 71
Leveraging ISO Settings for Exposure Adjustment 72

CHAPTER NINE 74
MOVIE SHOOTING 74

Basic Movie Recording Operation 74
Types of Video Files 77
Types of Tone Modes 78
ISO Settings for Movie Recording 80

CHAPTER TEN 82
ADDRESSING COMMON Z8 TROUBLESHOOTING ISSUES 82

Battery Drains Rapidly 82
Blurry Images 82
Blackouts During Viewfinder Use 82
Autofocus Not Working Properly 83
Unable to Record Videos 83
Image Noise 83
The Camera is Slow in Performance 84
Camera Overheating 84
Images Not Transferring to Computer 84
Downloaded Images Appear Corrupted 84
Trouble getting your camera to focus on close-up subjects 85
Distorted Images 85
Accidental Setting Changes 85
Trouble with the touchscreen features 86
Conclusion 87

Chapter One
Introduction

At the core of the Z8 is an image sensor that seems to have been taken from the D850 and Z7 series, but it has much better internal bandwidth capabilities, which are primarily made possible by the stacked sensor architecture, but with some adjustment of the BSI side. Regarding the sensor's technical specifications, Nikon has remained silent, but testing and close inspection indicate that this is most likely the Z7 II BSI bits combined with extra hardware in the ADC and stacking parts, along with some more unused photosites for an unknown purpose (possibly black level balancing).

Nikon did adjust the analog gain and read noise of this new picture sensor, most likely as a result of operating quicker transistors. However, the Z8 image sensor's pixel-level performance seems to indicate that the huge well size of the photodiode on top is the same as the D850/Z7 one. Additionally, the autofocus implementation on the sensor is identical to that of the Z7 II: the dual focus/image function is performed, as before, in every twelfth blue/green row of photosites.

The Z8 image sensor seems to have been designed with the express purpose of increasing the speed at which data is moved off the sensor. Additionally, a simplification occurred throughout that process: it seems like the Z8 sensor just transfers 14-bit data for still images. For JPEG or NEF files, there is no ADC circuit modification available to produce different bit depths from the whole picture data. The Z8 image sensor's working principle is essentially to gather data and transfer it off the top of the sensor stack as quickly as possible while generating as little extra noise as possible (speed is usually equated with noise in sensor designs). Additionally, the Z8 has 64–25600 ISO capability, with Lo or Hi settings available for 32, 50, 51200, and 102400. The dual gain image sensor has an ISO 500 change point.

The upgraded EXPEED7 image processor is paired with the new, quick image sensor. EXPEED has always been based on the current Socionext SoC (system on a chip), which is a chip that is descended from the original Fujitsu Milbeaut processor that Nikon utilized. These processors are based on ARM cores, much like your smartphone, but they also feature extra hardware from Nikon and other sources, as well as a built-in GPU and video CODEC, which power additional functionality. We do know, however, that the EXPEED7 is equipped with at least one more new engine, licensed from intoPIX, which powers a large portion of its high-end video and high-efficiency NEF capabilities in addition to providing us with HEIF files. Now available in 6/7nm manufacturing sizes, Socionext falls under the Qualcomm SnapDragon category.

Two 120Hz data pipelines (which produce the 120 fps focus data stream and the 120 fps maximum frame rate) are located between the image sensor and the EXPEED7 microprocessor. The standard image processing chain is reached via the first pipeline. A new viewfinder and focus processing chain are used in the second.

One of the Z8's primary physical features is made possible by its speed and twin pipelines: a nearly real-time, blackout-free viewfinder that eliminates the need for a mechanical shutter. This is a result of the Z8's lack of a mechanical shutter. Alternatively, electronic shutter speeds ranging from 15 minutes to 1/32,000 second are available. Flash sync speed is just 1/200, however.

Despite having a rolling shutter, the Z8's electronic shutter is very quick. According to Nikon, it is comparable in speed to a mechanical shutter operating at a 1/250 flash sync speed, which is the rate at which a mechanical shutter switches from full frame exposure to slit-scan exposure.

Furthermore, certain LED displays and lights have timing problems that might interfere with the speed of the electronic shutter. Thankfully, Nikon included high-frequency flicker reduction in the Z8, so you can select non-standard shutter speeds in as short as 1/96 EV increments (usually we can only go as little as 1/3EV). However, in certain cases, you'll have to experiment to find the ideal shutter speed.

Additionally, vehicles (body, front, detail), aircraft (body, front, cockpit), animals (body, head, eyes), and humans (torso, face, eyes) may all be automatically detected and focused on by the Z8. It's important to realize that there is a hierarchy involved in each of the topics the Z8 can detect— yes, animals include birds. Occasionally, you may see this in action when the camera determines what to focus on (in an all-automatic setting). Depending on how sure the camera is in what it finds, the Z8 may display a box on an animal's body, then narrow that to the face, then narrow that even more to the eyes. All of this may happen in a matter of milliseconds or immediately.

All four sizes of Auto-area AF and Wide-area AF are compatible with automatic subject detection. In the meanwhile, the three sizes of Pinpoint, Single-point AF, and Dynamic-area AF all locate a focus point using more conventional direct phase detection techniques. The reintroduction of 3D-tracking, which combines pattern/color matching and subject identification, is a wonderful feature. Unlike with the earlier mirrorless Nikons, there is no need to choose between tracking mode and default mode.

We now have a few additional direct AF-area modes, button-toggle choices, and the reintroduction of the AF-ON+AF-area mode, so you may now customize your camera to a broad variety of "hybrid focus" approaches. AF-ON, DISP, and thumb stick push are the three autofocus control buttons that you may have at your right thumb tip when combined with the option to reprogramme the DISP button to a focus function.

At the highest "normal" frame rate of 20 frames per second for still photography, the camera receives six frames of focus data for each frame taken since the focus system typically supplies information at a rate of 120 frames per second. This aids in the Z8's superior tracking of moving objects. Given that we're talking about frame rates for still images, the fact that the Z8 "doesn't work at 30 fps, like the Sony A1 does" is one of its "controversial" features. They do, however, only for JPEG files. Additionally, the Z8 can record full frame, reduced-size 11mp files at 120 frames per second and 19mp DX files at 60 frames per second. Its only restriction is that the files must be JPEGs and it has no control over focus, exposure, or lens. It should be noted that the camera may catch activity up to one second before you hit the shutter release and preserve those buffered photographs with images taken after the shutter release is pushed with these three "fast" frame rates (30, 60, and 120). Consequently, with the Z8, the days of not seeing the bird on a stick flying flight are over.

More frame rate options are available to you than what the 20, 30, 60, and 120 figures imply. You have the option to choose 1, 2, 3, 4, 5, 6, 8 (really 7.5) and 10 frames per second for low continuous and 10, 12, 15, and 20 frames per second for high continuous. Keep in mind that all of those numbers virtually split into 120, meaning there is no blackout in the viewfinder for any of them.

The fact that all of those speeds can also be quiet makes them much more intriguing. It's true that the Z8's "shutter sound" is entirely electronic and simulates a mechanical shutter. Taking pictures without the noise from the camera is a little unsettling. In addition to activating the fake shutter sound, you may activate two distinct edge line patterns in the viewfinder that appear when a picture is captured, or an imitation blackout (don't worry, it doesn't entirely black out; it truly simply dims between frames).

Also, you may limit the shutter sound to just play on headphones. Though this can affect frame rates, you can set the Z8 in Silent mode if you don't want the camera to make any noise at all, including VR, focus, and aperture sounds—

not that those are noticeable. Moreover, flash cannot be used in silent mode. But be aware that the VR sled beneath the sensor will lock and produce noise if the camera times out while the VR is on.

The body of the Z8 is, of course, one of its key components. The Z8 has a hybrid body structure. The lens mount, VR sled, and image sensor are attached to the magnesium alloy front frame of the camera. Sereebo, a polymer with carbon fiber woven into it, makes up the remainder of the camera frame. Hence, the frame/shell weighs less and is just as durable as metal since it is continuous under all surfaces. Also, according to Nikon, the Z8 and Z9 have equivalent levels of weather sealing. There is a seal behind every joint and gap (for controls).

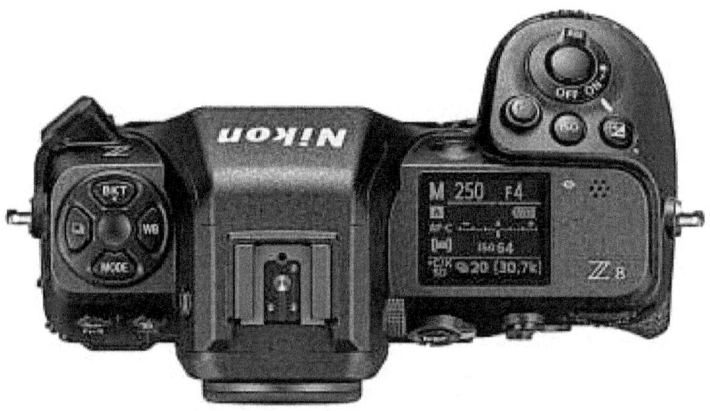

As we move around the body, you should see the top section of the camera: a cluster of buttons to the left of the viewfinder, a settings display to the right, and the now "standard" arrangement of three buttons directly behind the shutter release. The flash button has been replaced with a WB (white balance) button.

The return of the two-button fast instructions (reset and format card) will be noticeable to keen viewers. The two buttons with a green dot next to them are for resetting, and the two buttons with the red Format sub-labels are for formatting.

Unfortunately, the hot shoe above the viewfinder is merely a hot shoe exclusive to Nikon. Since Canon and Sony have recently added to their flagship cameras, there isn't a dedicated digital port on the front. Don't give up; Tascam has previously created an audio attachment that makes use of the 3.5mm microphone port to provide power for XLR microphones if necessary.

The Z8's rear should be quite recognizable. It has the Z9 button locations combined with the Z6/Z7 button simplicity. Just like the Z6/Z7, Nikon introduced the Z8 and the Z System controls, which are now combined with the controls from the previous DSLR flagship models.

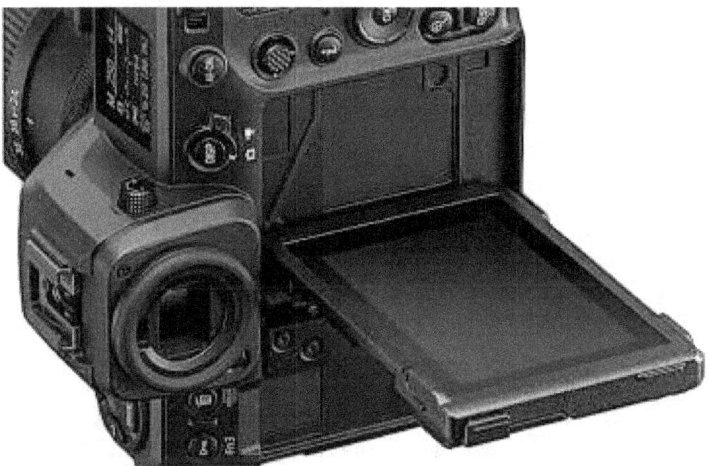

The EN-EL15C, the latest version of the conventional smaller battery, powers the Z8. Yes, you can use the majority of earlier EN-EL15s with the Z8, however only the B and C models can be charged over USB in the camera. Note that the original EN-EL15s, which were not marked as Lion20, would not function in the Z8. According to Nikon, the Z8 is compatible with EN-EL15A, EN-EL14B, and EN-EL15C batteries.

There is a new NETWORK menu with options to connect to additional cameras, computers, smart devices, and FTP. If you want to go deep into that menu and set up the Z8 to connect to your preferred whatever, get ready to nerd out. It may need some setup trial and error, but it is possible.

The WR-R11a wireless transmitter (as well as the previous WR-R10 model) and other vintage remote-control alternatives are supported via the conventional 10-pin circular connector on the front of the camera. Moreover, external GPS devices are supported. Nikon has reoriented the 10-pin connection such that it is oriented diagonally, which makes accessing the lock-down rings somewhat simpler than it was on prior models.

Furthermore, the following are the basic video capabilities of the camera: Full HD 24/25/30/50/60/100/120, 4K 24/25/30/50/60/100/120, and 8K 24/25/30. The Z8 also provides three basic video compressions (ProRes 4:2:2HQ, H.265, and H.264; which one is accessible depending on the frame size and frame rate you specify) and internal 10-bit recording. A filmmaker can record in resolutions up to 8K/50/60 and 12-bit resolution using ProRes RAW or Nikon RAW (.NEV files) on the Nikon Z8. You should use caution while recording in raw, however, since doing so might cause the camera to overheat in 8K. Of fact, you may run out of card space first, given the volume of data being created.

Nikon has also included some mind-blowing video capabilities in the Z8, such as the waveform display, in addition to raw footage. As a top-up to peak-level zebras, the Z8 also offers mid-tone zebras, which are helpful in many broadcast circumstances since they show you where the majority of the signal is being placed within the optimal tonal range.

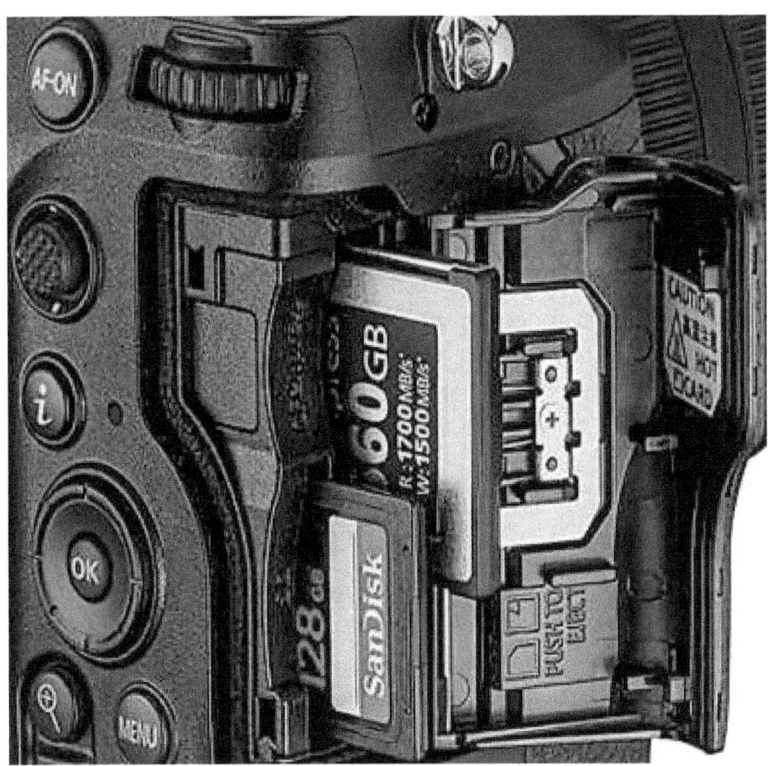

The Z8 has two card slots for storing images and videos. The top slot supports XQD or CFexpress Type B cards, while the bottom slot accepts SD (UHS-II compliant) cards. Nikon offers all of the standard dual-slot features that it has in the past, such as JPEG main — JPEG secondary (which lets you rapidly make a large JPEG and a little JPEG for pushing off the camera via SnapBridge or another connection).

Chapter Two
Getting Started with Your Camera

If you want to start using your camera, here's a simple guide to setting up your camera: start by charging the battery, then attach the lens, insert a memory card, and sync the clock. However, for beginners exploring the world of photography, it is crucial to become proficient in navigating the menu button, command dials, and touch screen. Mastering these essential skills will guarantee the accurate configuration of your camera during the initial setup phase.

Important Buttons and Controls for the Camera Initial Setup

Before you begin capturing moments with your Z8 camera, there's a detailed checklist that requires your attention. It involves familiarizing yourself with the complexities of different camera controls that are utilized for configuring the camera, such as the menu and multi-selector buttons. Let us see these controls, shedding light on their roles and functionalities:

1. The Menu Button: This is located on the left side of the LCD panel, providing access to a wide range of settings and options. With just a touch, you'll effortlessly navigate through the menus. A quick press will either confirm your choice or take you back to where you started, depending on the situation.

2. The Multi-Selector: With its central hub and ergonomically sized satellites, this control resembles the ones found on point-and-shoot wonders and other cameras. Providing expert guidance in navigating menus, focusing on specific options, and seamlessly reviewing images, it effortlessly directs you in all directions, ensuring a smooth and intuitive experience.

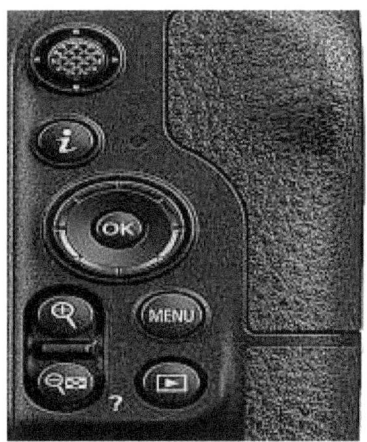

3. The Multi-Selector Button: This is the key player in your menu navigation, seamlessly guiding you through its various options. With its versatility and finesse, this device seamlessly adapts to any situation, making it a reliable choice.

4. The "OK" Button: A reliable ally in the world of confirmation, this button is unmatched in its ability to solidify agreements. Although its main functions are focused on playback and navigating between card domains, it remains a reliable and consistent tool during constant change.

5. The Sub-Selector Control: Designed with utmost precision for fine-tuning focus, this control possesses hidden capabilities that go beyond navigating menus. With a skilled touch, it can effortlessly capture the perfect focus and exposure, silently preserving the essence of your vision.

6. The Main Command and Sub Command Dials: They are strategically positioned at the front and back of the Z8, giving them immense control over the settings. The main control dial is at the forefront, orchestrating the interplay of shutter speeds, while its sub-counterpart plays a complementary role, adjusting secondary elements with precision. Mastering the art of Manual exposure mode requires a deep understanding of the sub-command dial for aperture adjustment and the main command dial for controlling shutter speed. Mastering the Z8's exposure meter brings these dials to life, turning them into powerful tools for creative control. And if the meter falls asleep, a soft press of the shutter release button awakens it, bringing back balance to the array of settings.

Navigating the Touchscreen

The tilting LCD on your camera offers more than just a way to view your shots. It's a versatile tool that allows photographers of all levels to explore a range of touch-enabled features and unleash their creativity. With its intuitive interface, the touchscreen allows for easy setup and smooth navigation. Below is the range of functions and capabilities it offers:

Playback Mode:

- **Navigating Through Images**: Effortlessly glide through your image gallery with swipe gestures, easily reliving moments at your fingertips.

- **Zooming in Images**: Explore the intricate details with precision by effortlessly adjusting magnification levels using a pinch or spread gesture.

- **Adjusting the Magnified Area**: Effortlessly change your viewpoint by swiping across the screen to reposition the zoomed-in area.

- **Accessing Thumbnails and Movies**: Effortlessly navigate through thumbnails and videos, using intuitive tapping and swiping gestures to reveal your precious visual memories.

Live View Mode:

This is a feature that allows you to view and capture images using the display screen on your camera. It provides a convenient and user-friendly way to compose your shots, making it easier to capture the perfect image.

- **Take Photos:** Simply touch to capture, eliminating the need to search for the shutter button. Experience the magic of capturing moments as they happen.
- **Focus Point Selection:** Easily choose your desired focal point on the screen for precise focusing.
- **Perfecting White Balance:** Enhance your color palette by pinpointing a specific area on the display to calculate the ideal white balance.

Shooting Modes:

- **Navigating through Menus:** Navigate through menus with ease. Effortlessly navigate through your shooting experience with the help of user-friendly touchscreen controls.
- **Inputting Texts:** Inputting text has never been easier. Master the art of seamless data entry with the intuitive on-screen keyboard, allowing you to effortlessly input everything from copyright information to personalized settings.

Note: Touch features are highly customizable, allowing you to shape them to your liking. Customize them to your preferences or disable them completely, giving you the flexibility to optimize your workflow. With customizable full-frame playback "flicks" and the ability to disable Touch Shutter/AF in live view and video recording, you have even more flexibility and control at your fingertips.

How to Use Touchscreen Gestures:

- **The Flick Gesture:** Effortlessly glide through your gallery with a swift swipe, smoothly transitioning between images.
- **The Slide Gesture:** Effortlessly navigate through magnified images by sliding your finger across the screen in any direction.

- **The Stretch/Squeeze Gesture**: Easily adjust the image size to your liking by using a simple pinch or spread gesture, giving you full control over your view.

- **The Tap Gesture**: Easily interact with precision by tapping to select, customize, or focus, seamlessly integrating touch into your shooting experience.

Language Selection

The Z8 camera is designed to be user-friendly and accessible to photographers all around the world, regardless of language barriers. With its extensive language support, the camera's interface offers a smooth and personalized experience, catering to your preferred language. Here's a step-by-step guide to help you customize the language settings:

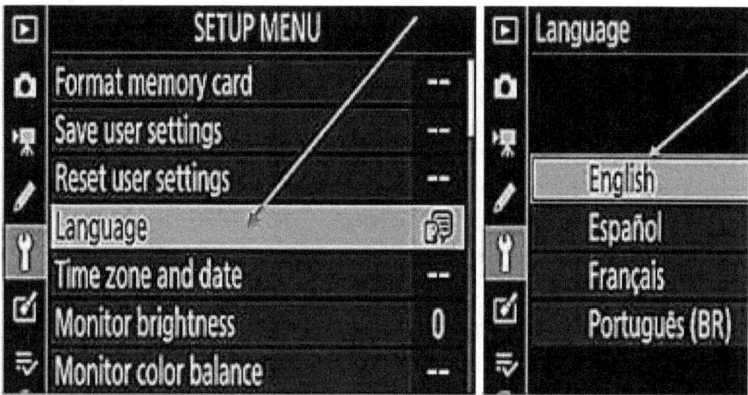

Go to the Setup Menu: Discover the Setup Menu by navigating to the Setup menu on your Z8 camera. This menu is the ultimate hub for all your configuration options, providing a wide range of settings to personalize your shooting experience.

Select the Language Option: When you enter the Setup Menu, you'll need to search for the Language option, which can be a bit tricky to locate. Explore the menu options, navigating through the digital interface until you come across this important setting.

Use the Multi-selector Pad: Utilize the circular Multi-selector pad located at the back of the camera. With expert skill, navigate through the wide selection of languages, effortlessly scrolling in all directions with precision.

Make Sure You've Made the Right Choice: Now that you've found the perfect language from the vast array of options, it's time to finalize your decision. To confirm your selection, you can press either the OK button located at the bottom left corner of the camera or the Multi-selector center button positioned at the center of the pad.

Note: The camera's language settings are typically pre-configured by distributors to align with regional preferences. However, if you're looking to switch to a different language, these simple steps will help you make a smooth transition and add a personal touch to your camera experience.

Configuring Time Zone and Date

It is important to have your Z8 camera synchronized with the correct time zone for a smooth photographic experience. Follow these detailed instructions to set your camera's location with precision:

Heading to the Setup Menu: Begin your adventure by exploring the Setup Menu. Explore the digital maze until you arrive at the third screen, where a plethora of settings are ready for your personalization. This menu is the ultimate hub for fine-tuning every aspect of your camera's functionality.

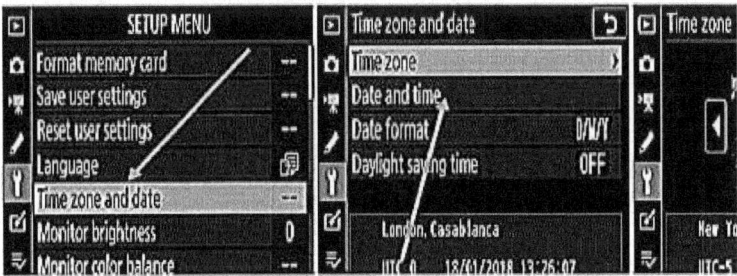

Changing the Time Zone:

- **Use the Multi Selector Pad**: Take advantage of the Multi Selector Pad to navigate smoothly through the menu options. Discover your current location, highlighted in a vibrant shade of yellow. This visual indicator, along with a vertical stripe or subtle outline, and a red dot, indicates the chosen time zone. Make sure to double-check the time zone displayed in the bottom-right corner of the screen for accuracy.

- **Verify What You Have Selected**: Once you have made your decision on the time zone, simply press the OK icon to confirm your option. You'll notice that your camera's internal clock is now perfectly synchronized with the world around you. Now that your time zone is set, you're ready to go through the steps of configuring date and time settings.

Configuring the Date and Time:

- **Return to the Third Screen**: Go back to the third screen in the Setup Menu to configure the date and time.

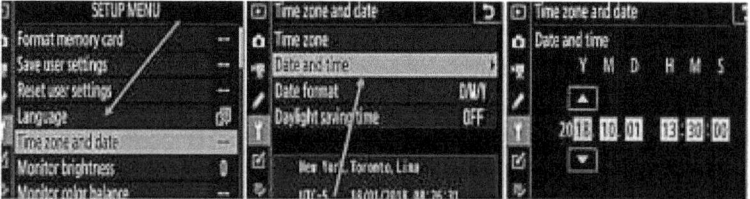

- **Fine-tune with the Multi Selector**: Use the Multi Selector pad to easily navigate between sections containing dates and times. Make precise adjustments by moving vertically or horizontally to fine-tune the parameters. Embrace the military time format for precise and meticulous recording of the date and time.

- **Double-check Your Settings**: Once you've carefully entered your date and time, simply press the OK button to save your configurations. Ensuring that your camera's internal clock is perfectly synchronized with the specified date and time in your chosen time zone is crucial for flawless operation.

Changing the Date and Time Format:

- **Return to the Setup Menu:** Go back to the Setup Menu and look for the third screen again.

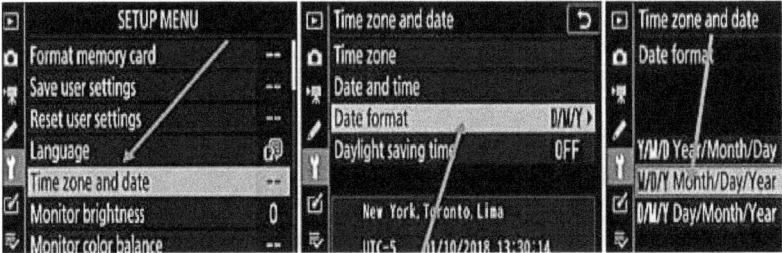

- **Navigate and Customize:** Use the Multi Selector pad to easily move through the options and choose your desired date format from the wide range of choices available.

- **Verify Your Selection:** Finalize your choice by pressing the OK button, and customizing the date and time display to suit your personal preferences.

Powering Up: Battery Installation and Charging

Keeping your camera's battery fully charged is necessary for a smooth photography experience with your Nikon Z8. With efficient power management, you can shoot without any interruptions, giving you the freedom to focus on capturing that perfect shot. Follow the steps below to learn how to charge and install your battery:

Charging Process:

- When the battery is inserted into the MH-25a charger, a comforting pulse of light lets you know that the charging process has begun.

- As the charging process progresses, the indicator light gently pulses for around 2.5 hours, indicating that the battery is absorbing vital energy.

- When the battery is fully charged, the status indicator emits a steady glow to let you know that the charging cycle is complete.

How to Insert the Battery into the Camera:

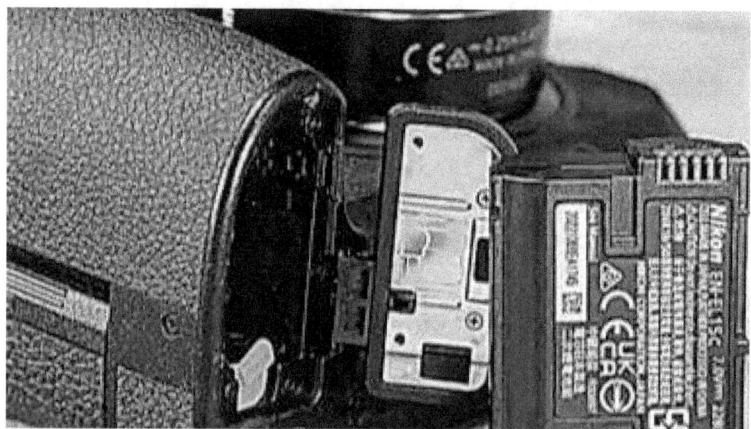

- Now that the charging process is finished, it's time to smoothly incorporate the refreshed battery into your Z8 camera.

- Gain access to the camera's battery compartment by gently opening the lever located on the underside, revealing the gateway to power.

Attaching the Lens

Getting your Nikon Z8 camera ready for action with your preferred lens is easy. Here are some easy steps to handle your lens and make sure it's securely attached for safe shooting:

Unpacking the Lens: Carefully take the lens out of its packaging, ensuring that the rear lens cover is in place to provide extra protection against dust and scratches.

Storing the Lens for Easy Access: Place the lens in the designated compartment of your camera case, ensuring it is inserted vertically. This not only makes it convenient to grab when necessary but also protects against unintended harm.

Getting Ready for Installation: Rotate the body cover away from the release mechanism and remove both the rear lens cover and the body cap, setting them aside for later use.

Installing the Lens:

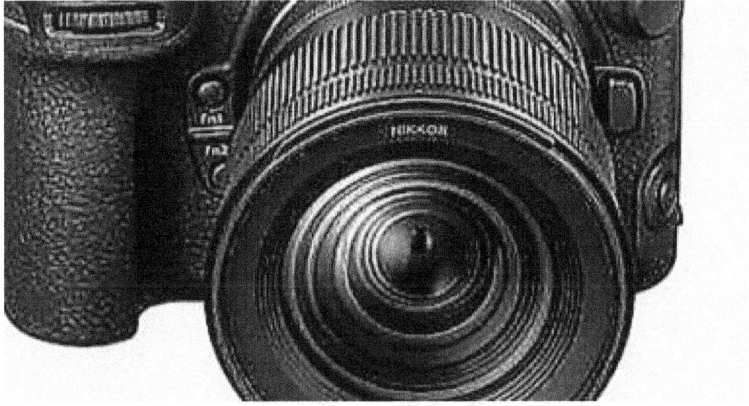

- Make sure to align the raised white protrusion on the lens mount with the corresponding indication on the lens barrel.

- Rotate the lens until you hear a secure click, making sure it's aligned correctly with the direction of the shutter release button.

- Certain lenses, particularly telephotos or those with swiveling collars, may need additional attention when being installed. Make sure to adjust the collar to avoid any collisions between the tripod foot and the camera's prism front overhang. This will ensure a perfect fit.

Enabling Autofocus: To enable autofocus functionality after attaching the lens, simply switch the focus mode to either M-AF or AF.

How to Attach the Lens Hood: For enhanced portability and to reduce any unwanted light flare, try reversing the lens hood and adjusting the "petals" to face outward. This also helps to shield the front portion of the lens from any potential disruptions.

Adjusting Diopter Settings

Fine-tuning the viewfinder of your camera can have a significant impact on capturing the ideal shot, particularly for those passionate about photography. If you're already familiar with wearing glasses or contact lenses, you may not have to adjust the diopter correction settings. For individuals who enjoy shooting without glasses, the Z8 offers a convenient built-in diopter adjustment feature to accommodate your needs.

You can adjust the diopter within a range, allowing you to finely tune the focus through the viewfinder and achieve exceptional image clarity. Just take a peek through the viewfinder and adjust the diopter until the image looks sharp and clear. Remember, when checking focus through the viewfinder, rely on your judgment based on the actual image rather than the indicators outside. Occasionally, the distance between the focus screen and the indicators may vary, which can impact the accuracy of focus.

Now, if you're someone who knows a lot about cameras, it's useful to remember your settings when you share your camera with others who have different diopter preferences. With this method, switching back to your preferred diopter is a breeze, saving you the trouble of readjusting each time. Take note of the number of turns and twists required to switch between users, making the process more efficient for everyone involved.

If the standard diopter correction range doesn't fully meet your requirements, Nikon provides a selection of nine diopter-adjustment viewfinder correction lenses to cater to your specific needs. These lenses offer additional customization options, enabling you to adjust your viewing experience according to your individual visual preferences. Prices start at approximately $16, guaranteeing photography sessions that are tailored to your needs, providing clear and comfortable results.

Installing a Memory Card

Follow the steps below to learn how to insert a memory card:

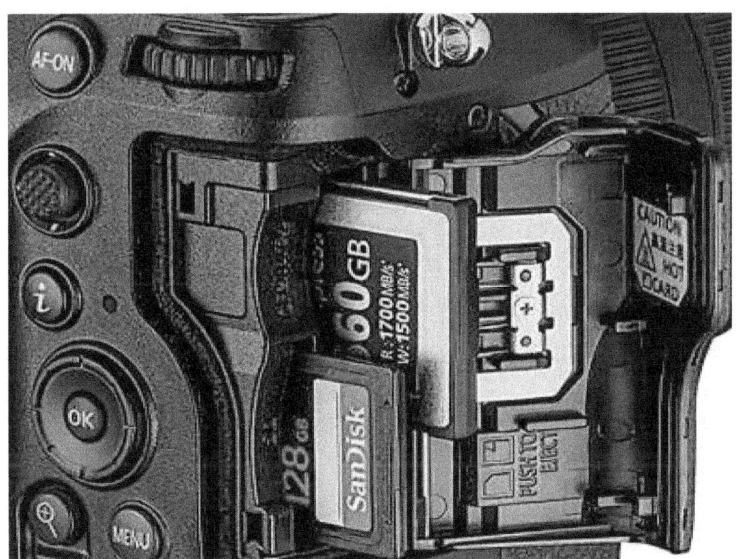

- Initiate the process by unlatching the memory card cover. This can be done by delicately sliding the door located on the rear-right side of the camera towards the device's rear, proceeding with caution as you open it.

- Before proceeding, ensure that the camera is either powered off or that the memory access indicator, indicating ongoing card writing activities, remains unlit. This precautionary measure is indispensable in preventing potential data corruption or loss.
- Inside the memory card compartment, you'll find two card slots, an **XQD card** slot positioned at the lower section and an **SD media** slot situated at the upper part.
- Verify that the label on the XQD card faces toward the camera's rear during insertion. Introduce the card into the slot with the edge bearing the contacts leading the way. This guarantees precise alignment and a seamless connection.
- Once proper alignment is confirmed, gently and smoothly slide the card into place until it audibly clicks, indicating secure insertion.

Now, see the steps to safely remove the memory card from your camera:

- Before you start the removal process, ensure that the camera is powered off or that the memory access indicator remains unilluminated.
- Subsequently, locate and remove the desired memory card for removal. For an XQD card, simply press it inward, prompting it to pop out for easy removal.
- Exercise caution to handle the card with care, mitigating any potential damage to the contacts or the card itself.
- When removing an SD card, gently push it inward until it springs out, and then meticulously take it out from the slot.

Chapter Three

Going Over the Camera External Buttons and Controls

Top Side Controls and Features

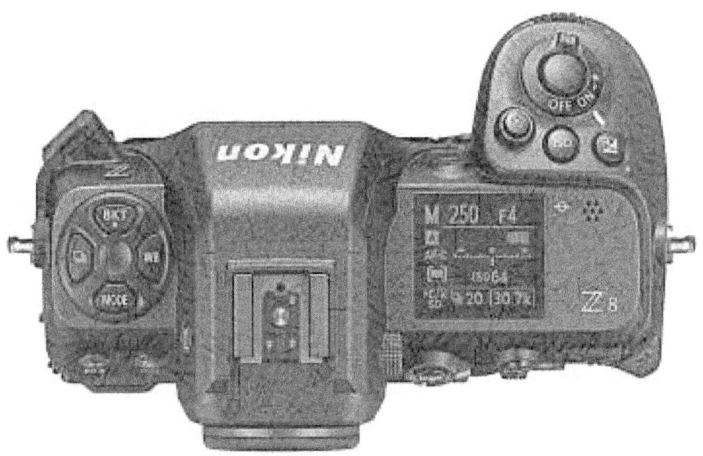

BKT Bracketed Button: To take bracketed pictures, use the BKT Bracket Button along with the Main Command Dial and the Sub-Command Dial. This combination lets you change the number of frames and the difference in brightness between each shot.

White Balance Button: Pressing the WB button will bring up the white balance settings. Turn either the Main Command Dial or the Sub-Command Dial to move through the choices until you find the white balance you want.

Microphone: Take advantage of the stereo mics with two channels for recording videos. These mics provide better sound quality during video meetings, which makes watching more enjoyable overall.

Movie Recording Button: When your camera is in video mode, press the "video record" button to easily start and stop recording, making it easy to catch every important scenario.

Shutter Release Button: Partially pressing the camera release button starts focusing, and completely pressing it takes the picture.

ON and OFF Button: Easily control the camera's power level with the "On/Off" button, switching between active and sleep modes as needed.

ISO Button: You can change the ISO level by hitting the ISO button and turning the main command wheel. This lets you adapt to different lighting situations and get the best brightness.

Exposure Compensation Button: You can fine-tune the exposure settings by pressing the main command key and the exposure correction button at the same time. This will make sure that your photos have accurate and balanced exposure levels.

Speaker: Use the camera's speaker to play back audio, which makes it easier to listen to settings and alerts and to review sounds that have been caught.

Control Panel: You can quickly get to the camera's fixed settings through the control panel, which makes it easy to get important shooting information.

Diopter Adjustment Control: With the diopter adjustment, you can change the focus of the lens to fit your eyesight. This will make sure that you can see clearly and comfortably.

The Monitor Mode Button: You can go between the camera and monitor screens via this button, allowing you to choose the display mode that works best for your shooting needs.

Shooting Mode Button: By hitting the mode button and turning the Main Command Dial, you can easily switch between shooting modes. Programmed Auto, Aperture

Priority, Shutter Speed Priority, and Manual are the modes that can be used.

Release Mode Button: You can get better control over shot speed and timing by using the release mode button and the Main Command Dial together to change the setting on the Release Mode Dial.

Back View Controls and Features

The back buttons on your camera can help you do a lot of different things. Let's see how they work:

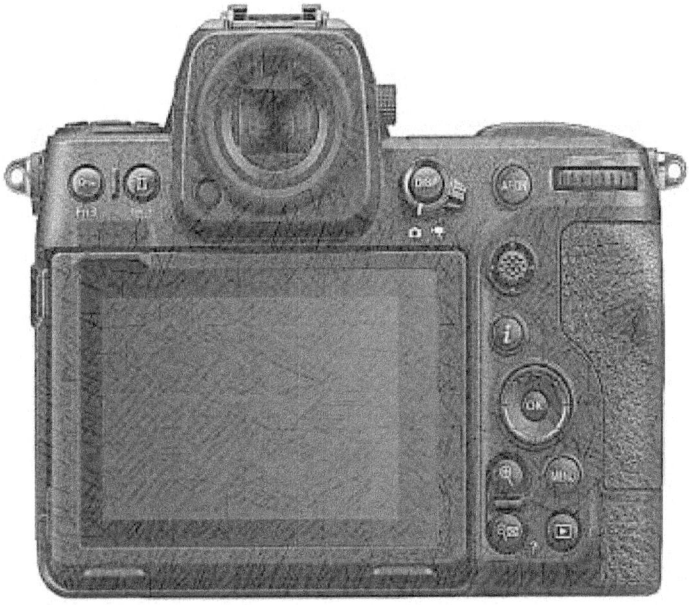

Eye Sensor: When you look through the lens, the eye sensor knows and changes the display from computer to camera without you even noticing. Put away those awkward switches!

Display Switcher Button: Press the DISP button to switch between different display panels and make your screen fit the way you shoot and your tastes.

Mode Shifter Button: This button makes it easy to switch between photo and video modes, so you're always ready to record the moment, whether it's in still or moving pictures.

Focus Point Navigator Joystick: The sub-selector joystick lets you fine-tune how focus points are used. When you need to, press and hold to lock the brightness and focus settings.

Autofocus Activator Button: Clicking the AF-ON button starts autofocus, which makes sure that objects are sharp and close-ups are perfect.

Parameter Adjustment Dial: The main command dial makes it easy to change camera settings like aperture, shutter speed, and exposure, giving you full control over your shots.

Quick Menu Access Button: Pressing the iButton will quickly take you to the camera's menu settings, where you can make changes right away to suit your needs.

OK Button: Press the "OK" button to confirm your menu options and settings and make sure your camera works the way you want it to.

Multi-selector: Using the multi-selector button, you can easily move through options and choose where to focus by navigating them without any problems.

Image Zoom Magnifier: The enlarge button lets you make images on the LCD screen bigger, so you can look at them more closely and more closely.

Menu Button: Clicking the menu button ushers you to the camera menu settings, where you can modify a lot of the camera's settings.

Image Viewing Zoom-out Button: Zoom out to get a closer look at pictures on the LCD screen, which makes reviewing and judging images more thorough.

Instant Image Review Playback Button: The playback button lets you quickly look over the most recent picture on the LCD screen, so you're always up to date on your shots.

Image Deletion Trash Button: Use the trash button to get rid of useless photos from the camera's memory, making room for new photo projects.

Image Protection Button: The Protect/Fn3 button lets you keep important pictures from being deleted or changed by accident, and it gives you control over the picture quality and style settings.

Front View Controls and Features

Learn about the different buttons and settings on the front of your camera. Each one has a specific job to do:

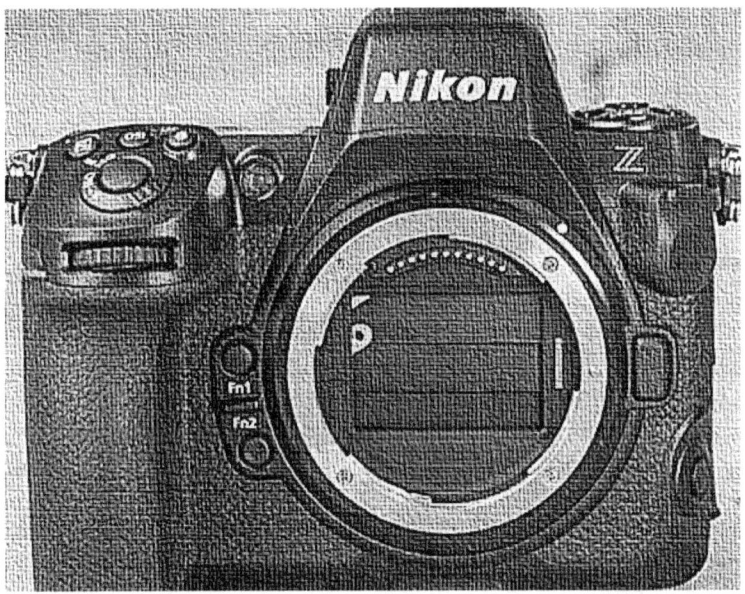

Sub-Command Dial for Versatile Settings Adjustment: The sub-command dial allows you to tweak various camera settings and options, granting you enhanced freedom and control while capturing your moments.

10-Pin Remote Terminal (Located beneath the Lid/cover): Beneath the lid lies the 10-pin remote connector, where additional remote controls can be joined, enabling remote release and control of the camera from a distance.

External Microphone Connector (under the Side Cover): Concealed beneath the side cover, this port facilitates the seamless connection of external microphones, elevating the quality of sound capture during video recording or audio capture sessions.

Headphone Jack for Real-time Audio Monitoring: Tucked away on the side of the camera, the headphone port allows for the connection of external headphones. This enables real-time monitoring of recordings, ensuring meticulous scrutiny of sound quality and volume.

HDMI Connector (Positioned under the Side Cover): Housed beneath the side cover, the HDMI port facilitates the connection of an HDMI cable. This enables the transmission of high-definition video to external computers or screens.

USB Data Connector for Seamless Data Transfer: Hidden under the side cover, the USB data port enables the connection of a data cable for effortless file and data transfer between the camera and a computer or other compatible device

USB Power Plug for Continuous Power Supply: Also nestled under the side cover, the USB power port functions in tandem with a USB power supply cable, ensuring the camera remains powered up during extended shooting sessions or data transfer operations.

Focus Mode Button for Focus Mode Selection: Click on the focus mode button to access and adjust the focus mode settings. Then, utilize the Main Command Dial to tailor the settings to suit your shooting preferences and requirements.

Battery Chamber Cover for Secure Battery Installation: The battery chamber cover provides access to the camera's battery compartment, ensuring safe and effortless installation of the battery, thereby enabling uninterrupted shooting sessions

Fn2 Button: The Fn2 button can be customized to perform specific functions by default, such as selecting the "Choose Image Area" option. This facilitates quick access to frequently used features or settings.

Fn1 Button: Similarly, the Fn1 button can be assigned a specific function, with the default option being the "Shooting Menu Bank," offering users easy control over the camera's functionality to align with their method of shooting.

Memory Card Slots: Found under the side cover, the memory card slots provide ample storage space for memory cards used to store photos and videos, ensuring you have abundant space to accommodate all your camera needs.

Chapter Four: How to Use the Camera Metering Modes

The Traditional Option: The 18% Gray Card:

It is best to use a well-lit exposure meter on a subject that reflects 18% of the incoming light for an accurate measurement of exposure. With accurate measurements guaranteed by this "middle-gray" reference point, most scenes—especially those with medium brightness—have ideal exposure. Also, for example, imagine a deep blue sky or verdant surroundings—ideal locations for calibrating.

When Midtones Become Difficult:

Extremely bright landscapes, such as snowy fields or volcanic rock formations, provide a problem for mid-tone metering; this is when using several strategies is helpful.

Your Palm: The Unexpected Substitute:

It may surprise you to learn that your palm may function as a surprisingly good gray card replacement. Even though reflectivity varies, using your palm as a guide often produces readings that are more accurate than those of a conventional gray card—but with a twist. You'll have to make up for it with an additional exposure stop.

To get the right exposure, for instance, if your meter indicates 1/500th sec at f/11, change it to either 1/200th sec at f/11 or 1/500th sec at f/8.

The Mini Gray Card:

Another choice is to get a little gray card that will slip into your camera bag easily. All you have to do is place the card close to your primary subject so that it faces the camera and is well-lit. Next, to get the most precise exposure measurement, use spot metering.

Note: Remember that many cameras are set up to record a slightly deeper gray than the typical Kodak gray card, which is around 12% reflectivity. This implies that to get the ideal balance, you may need to modify your exposure by half a stop above the meter reading.

Selecting the Right Metering Method

There is a powerful tool built into your camera that will work best if you know how to use its different modes. Here are some steps you can take to use its full potential:

Metering Modes:

The camera's light sensors can read light in four different ways:

Matrix Metering: The camera looks at the whole scene and adjusts the exposure so that the picture is well-exposed overall. This is the method that is used by default most of the time.

Center-Weighted Metering: The center of the frame is given more weight, which works well for pictures or objects that are in the middle of the design.

Spot Metering: This method lets you get the exact exposure you need for a particular subject, like a flower that stands out against a dark background because it only reads light from a small part of the screen.

Highlight-Weighted Metering: This type of metering focuses on keeping details in the highlights, which is helpful for scenes with lots of bright areas or great contrast.

Note: You can choose your favorite mode from the camera menu, or you can use Custom Setting f2 to make a button (Fn1 or Fn2) easier to reach. This means you don't have to go through settings to change between, say, spot metering for close-ups and center-weighted metering for photos. For everyday use, you can also leave the metering mode setting set to Matrix. Symbols in the lens make it easy to see which mode has been selected.

Learning How to Measure Light:

The sensor in the camera measures the light that comes in to figure out the exposure. From very dark (8 minutes at f/16) to very bright (1/1000 second at f/16), its range is very wide. This means that you can record light levels from a moonlit night (0 EV) to a snowfield bathed in sunlight (16 EV). But it's important to tell the difference between the sensor's dynamic range and its detecting range. The dynamic range is the range of tones that the camera can record, from bright to dark. The camera can pick up light that is farther away, but it can be hard to keep details in both bright spots and deep blacks.

Exploring the Various Metering Types

Matrix Metering

Imagine your camera as a scene detective; in Matrix Metering mode, it cracks the code of a well-lit image using a complex algorithm. Here's how it works:

Reading the Scene: Light Zones and Databases:

1. **Light Zones:** The camera analyzes the entire frame, dividing it into various sections. Each zone's brightness is compared to the overall light hitting the sensor (incident light).

2. **Database Detective:** This analysis is then compared against a vast database of over 30,000 images. By recognizing light distribution patterns, the camera can guess what you're shooting.

3. **Scene Interpretation:** For example, a much darker top half might suggest a sky-dominated landscape. Conversely, bright skin tones in the center could prioritize exposure for a portrait.

Matrix Metering's Strengths:
- **Versatility:** This "scene detective" approach works well in diverse lighting and subject scenarios.
- **Convenience:** It often delivers accurate exposure with minimal adjustments, especially for portraits with balanced lighting.

When Matrix Metering Needs Help:
- **Low Light or Overcast Skies:** In these situations, the camera might underexpose, resulting in darker-than-ideal images.

Modern Metering Goes Beyond Brightness:

Modern cameras add more data to the exposure equation, making Matrix Metering even smarter:

1. **Pattern Recognition:** The camera identifies recoverable details in shadows by comparing patterns across the sensor and referencing the database. This prioritizes highlight preservation, especially in RAW format.
2. **Color Analysis:** By recognizing green as foliage, skin tones as people, and blue as the sky, the camera refines exposure readings.
3. **Autofocus Focus:** The camera assumes your subject is what the autofocus has identified, further assisting exposure decisions.
4. **Lens Intelligence:** Information like focal length from Z-mount lenses helps the camera understand the scene better. Exposure adjustments are made differently for landscapes (wide-angle) versus portraits (telephoto).

Matrix Metering shines with its scene analysis and subject recognition. It can differentiate between high and low-contrast images, often slightly underexposing high-contrast scenes to preserve highlights. However, when using strong filters that alter light distribution (polarizing filters, for instance), center-weighted metering becomes a better option, as those filters can disrupt Matrix Metering's calculations

Center-weighted Metering

Imagine focusing on the most important part of your photo – that's the core idea behind center-weighted metering. Unlike earlier methods that averaged light across the entire frame, center-weighted metering prioritizes a specific zone in the center.

Developed before complex scene analysis techniques, this metering mode assumes your main subject is usually in the center of the picture. It gives more weight (around 75%) to the light reading in a central 12mm zone, while still considering the overall scene brightness (the remaining 25% influence).

How it Works:

Let's say your camera reads f/4 at 1/250 second for a properly exposed center subject, but the edges are darker and require f/16 at 1/250 second. Center-weighted metering would find a middle ground, suggesting an exposure around f/5.6 at 1/250 second, prioritizing the properly lit center.

Ideal Situations:

- **Central Subjects:** Center-weighted metering is perfect when your main subject – a person, flower, or any mid-toned object – is positioned in the center of the frame.
- **Portraits and Close-Ups:** This mode excels in these situations where the subject naturally occupies the center.

Limitations:
- **Bright or Dark Surrounds:** Large areas of extreme brightness or darkness around the center can throw off the metering, leading to less-than-ideal results.

The Benefit of Flexibility:

Many cameras offer different options for the metering area: the entire frame or the traditional 12mm center zone. This flexibility allows you to choose the mode that best suits your subject and lighting conditions.

For photographers who want balanced exposures without deep scene analysis, center-weighted metering is a valuable tool. It prioritizes your central subject while still considering the overall scene, making it a great choice for a variety of situations.

Spot Metering Mode

Spot metering is like having a tiny light meter built into your camera – perfect for photographers comfortable with handheld light meters who want precise control over exposure in specific areas.

What it Does:

- Measures light reflected from a tiny 4mm circle (1.5% of the frame) centered on the active focus point (not always the one displayed).
- Allows for accurate exposure readings on specific highlights, shadows, or mid-tones, regardless of the overall scene brightness.
- Offers more precise exposure control compared to matrix or center-weighted metering.

Ideal Situations:

- **High-contrast scenes:** When your subject is much brighter or darker than the background (like a white bird against a blue sky).

- **Off-center subjects:** You can adjust the metering point to ensure proper exposure for the main subject, even if it's not in the center.
- **Small, mid-toned subjects:** Get accurate readings for tiny subjects against contrasting backgrounds.

Important Considerations:

- **Manual correction might be needed:** Overexposed or underexposed areas can occur, especially with very bright or dark spots. Manual adjustments might be necessary for perfect results.

Using Spot Metering:

- **Requires specific focus modes:** Auto-area AF is the only mode that doesn't allow you to change the metering spot, which is always linked to the center focus point.
- **Choose an AF-area mode:** Select a mode that allows moving the focus point (check your camera's i menu).
- **Navigate the metering point:** Use the multi-selector to move the combined focus and metering point around the frame.
- **Auto-area AF limitations:** Spot metering still works in Auto-area AF, but with less flexibility as it uses the center point.

Remember:

- The focus point and metering point move together.
- Dynamic-area AF might shift the focus point (and metering area) during continuous focusing.

Highlight-weighted Metering

Imagine taking a picture of actors on stage. You want them to be perfectly exposed, but the dark background shouldn't affect their brightness. That's where highlight-weighted metering comes in.

Similar but Different:

- **Like Matrix Metering:** It analyzes the entire scene, similar to matrix metering, but with a specific focus.
- **Preserve Highlights:** Unlike spot metering (which uses the same icon with an asterisk), highlight-weighted metering prioritizes preventing blown-out highlights (areas with lost detail due to overexposure).

The Power of Dual Processors:

This mode relies on the camera's dual Expeed 6 processors to identify bright areas in your image. The camera then adjusts the exposure to ensure those highlights are captured correctly, even if it means slightly underexposing other areas.

Ideal Situations:

- **Scenes with Spread-Out Highlights:** This mode works well when bright areas are present across a significant portion of the frame, like actors under stage lights or a sunny landscape with snow.
- **Easier than Spot Metering:** Instead of manually aiming a tiny spot meter at the highlights (like with spot metering), highlight-weighted metering automates the process, prioritizing those bright areas for accurate exposure.

When it Works Best:

- **Clear Subject Separation:** This mode excels when the subject is distinct from the background. In our stage play example, the camera can differentiate between the actors (highlights) and the dark backdrop.

Locking Exposure for "Re-composition":

Once you've chosen your shutter speed, aperture, and ISO, getting the exposure right becomes crucial. Highlight-weighted metering allows you to recompose your shot (change the framing) without affecting the exposure settings you've locked in.

- **Locking the Exposure:** By default, pressing the center button on the multi-selector locks both exposure and focus (AE-L/AF-L).
- **Customizing the Lock Button:** You can use Custom Setting f2 to assign this function to another button, like the AF-ON button, for added convenience.

Choosing Your Lock Function:
- **AE Lock Only:** Locks exposure only, allowing you to refocus if needed.
- **AE/AF Lock (ideal with Back-Button Focus):** Locks both exposure and focus, perfect for situations like back-button focusing.

Managing Noise in Metering

Ever noticed that grainy, speckled appearance in some photos? That's image noise, and it's a photographer's nemesis (unless used for a special effect). Let's see what causes it and how to minimize it.

The Causes of Noise:
- **High ISO:** This setting boosts your camera's light sensitivity, great for low-light situations. But like cranking up the volume on a stereo, it amplifies not just the light (signal) but also unwanted electrical signals (noise). This becomes more noticeable at higher ISO values (typically ISO 800 and above). While some cameras handle high ISO better than others, noise is generally an enemy of clean, crisp images.
- **Long Exposures:** Longer exposure times allow more light to reach the sensor, but they also give the sensor more time to pick up heat as noise. Additionally, variations in the sensor itself can introduce fixed-pattern noise, especially in CMOS sensors like the one in the Z8.

Combating Noise in-Camera:

- **High ISO NR (Noise Reduction):** Your camera might have a noise reduction setting (usually High, Normal, Low, or Off) in the Photo Shooting menu. While it reduces noise, it can also soften the image, so use it judiciously. If preserving detail is crucial, consider keeping noise reduction off.

- **Long Exposure Noise Reduction:** For long exposures, the camera can take a second "dark" exposure with the shutter closed to identify noisy pixels. These pixels are then subtracted from the main image during processing. This can be helpful, but it may also reduce image detail.

Taking Control in Post-Processing:

Noise reduction software like Noise Ninja can be very effective in cleaning up noise from processed photos, especially RAW images. However, remember – less is often more. Apply noise reduction sparingly to avoid sacrificing image clarity.

Remember:

- While noise reduction tools exist, it's always better to prevent noise in the first place.

- Experiment with different ISO settings and exposure times to find the sweet spot between capturing light and minimizing noise.

- Consider using a tripod for long exposures to maintain image sharpness and reduce the need for extreme ISO settings.

Chapter Five
Harnessing the Power of HDR

Have you ever been enthralled by a scene and then annoyed by how starkly the highlights and shadows contrast when you try to photograph it? Once again, Nikon's clever Active D-Lighting (ADL) bracketing saves the day by guaranteeing the ideal exposure.

Releasing the Potential of Bracketing:

Imagine yourself in an amazing scene with deep, cold shadows in the valleys and snow-capped mountains drenched in sunshine. Under a typical exposure, the lowlands might seem completely black while the mountaintops are blown out (pure white). Here's where bracketing comes through. Nikon's bracketing mechanism records many, differently exposed images of the same scene. But ADL bracketing goes one further, deftly modifying the highlights and shadows in every picture to give it a more realistic appearance.

Getting Started with the Magic:

Use the wealth of possibilities found in the Photo Shooting Menu on your camera. The secret to releasing the power of ADL bracketing is to find the "Auto Bracketing Set" option. You may change each image's ADL settings and amount of shots here. Some Nikon models allow you to choose a specific Bracketing Burst button for extra convenience. As with exposure bracketing, you can quickly take a series of bracketed photos with a single push.

Navigating the Selections:

Let's analyze the particular choices at hand:

Zero Shots: Complete deactivation of ADL bracketing results. Conventional bracketing is still in use, however. Recall that, independent of bracketing settings, your selected ADL level

(Auto, Extra High, High, Normal, or Low) will still be applied to all of your photographs if you've enabled basic ADL in the Shooting Menu.

Two Shots: This records two pictures back to back. Taken using your chosen ADL setting, the first one is a control shot with ADL disabled. You may choose pairings like "Off/Auto" (applying Auto ADL to one shot and no ADL to the other) or particular pairings like "Off/Extra High," "Off/High," and so forth inside the "Amount" section.

Three-five shots: Here you may choose from three, four, or five photos. While the others will use the ADL settings you provide in the "Amount" section, one of them will be collected with ADL turned off. An interesting thing to remember is that the ADL parameters get established and cannot be changed via the "Amount" section once three, four, or five shots are taken:

Three Shots: This records pictures with ADL turned off, normal, and low.

Four Shots: This records pictures with the ADL options Off, Low, Normal, and High.

Five Shots: Images are taken with ADL settings of Off, Low, Normal, High, and Extra High.

Automatic HDR Functionality

Imagine that you are in a poorly lit room with a golden spotlight of sunshine coming through a window. The picture is arresting, with the subdued tones within and the colorful world outside in sharp contrast. But it seems unachievable to get it all in one camera shot. A quick shutter speed of 1/400th and a small aperture of around f/11 would be ideal for freezing the movement of the sunny landscape. But the inside needs more light, so even the newest cameras find it difficult to achieve a larger aperture (f/2.8) and a slower shutter speed (1/60th). Here is when inventive methods and dynamic range work their magic.

The Conundrum with Dynamic Range:

The limited dynamic range of digital cameras allows them to record a certain amount of light and shadow information. That limit is pushed over 7 f-stops by our scenario, which surpasses even the capabilities of a powerhouse like the z8. While significantly wider dynamic range sensors are in the future, for the time being, we have to depend on cutting-edge techniques like HDR (High Dynamic Range) photography and Active D-Lighting (ADL).

Activating HDR's Potential:

Photographers may take on high-contrast situations head-on with these methods. Both in-camera HDR and conventional bracketing are available with the z8.

The In-camera HDR: Without using extra software, this simple feature combines many exposures to produce a high-dynamic range picture from within the camera. It offers a three-stop/EV boost by combining two bracketed exposures taken in a single shot, much like a manual HDR. It's surprisingly good for daily usage even if it lacks the customization of conventional bracketing.

The Traditional HDR: Taking some bracketed exposures at different settings to cover the whole dynamic range is known as traditional HDR bracketing. Then, using specialist software such as Photomatix or Adobe's Merge to HDR, these exposures are blended. The finished picture properly captures the depth and contrast of the landscape with a much broader spectrum of tones. That's the good thing about HDR; a picture that combines a well-exposed inside with a vividly photographed outside.

Further Analysis on the In-Camera HDR

- **Access the Menu:** To see the Photo Shooting menu, press the Menu button (the camera icon).
- **HDR Settings:** Use the multi-selector button to get to the HDR area. Options for preserving individual

exposures, exposure differential, smoothing, and HDR mode are all found here.

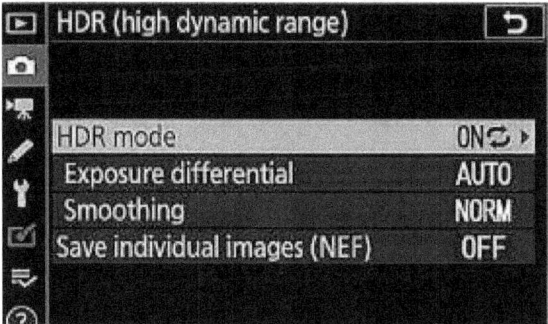

- To record one or more HDR photos, choose "On (single photo)" or "On (series)"; then, click "OK" to save your option.

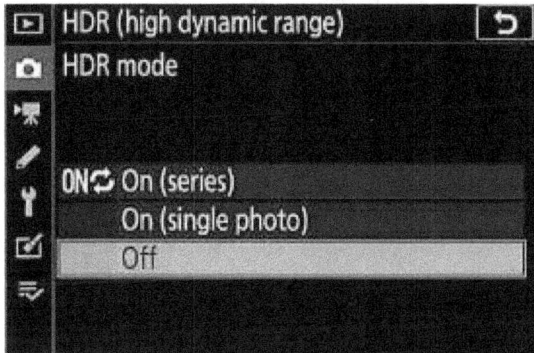

- Using the "Exposure Differential" option, which ranges from Auto to 3 EVs, fine-tune the contrast between exposures. Check by clicking "OK".

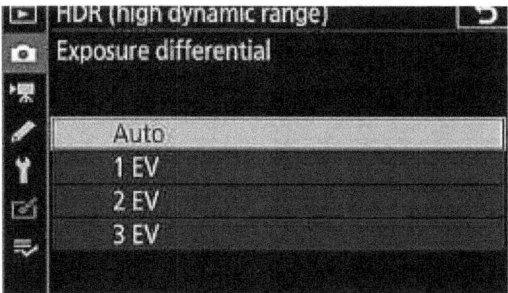

- **Smoothing Option**: By choosing "Smoothing" you may lessen any halo effects surrounding contrasting regions. Based on the impact you want, choose Normal, Low, or High.

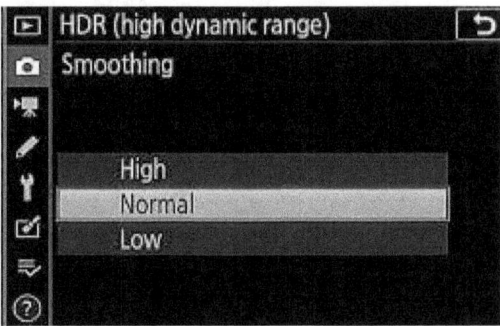

- **Preserve Individual Images (NEF)**: To preserve RAW copies of each taken exposure for further computer processing, turn on "Save Individual Images (NEF)".

- To regulate exposure by adjusting the f-stop while keeping your preferred depth-of-field, set your camera to Aperture-Priority mode.

- **Catch the Scene**: To reduce camera shaking, a tripod is strongly advised even when handheld filming is an option. Image alignment might be affected and cropping results with even little movement.

Utilizing Bracketing and Merge to HDR for Imaging

Although in-camera HDR is a fast fix, manual HDR gives you more flexibility and personalization that enhances your creative expression. Taking charge of the camera's algorithms, you carefully create the finished picture.

Bracketed Bursts' Power:

Manual HDR's secret is in taking many, varyingly light exposures of the same picture. With this method, called bracketing, you may get information in both the highlights (bright regions) and the shadows (dark areas) that a single exposure could overlook.

Assembling the Scene:

Manual HDR success is mostly upon preparation. You'll want the following:

A Sturdy Tripod: By serving as your anchor, a tripod guarantees less camera tremor between shots. The ultimate picture alignment might be upset by the tiniest movement.

Navigate to the bracketing options in the menu of your camera: Select a two or three-step EV bracketing interval. This guarantees a suitable range of exposures to grasp the whole dynamic range of the scene.

Turn on aperture priority on your camera: For depth-of-field control, this enables you to choose an aperture and stick with it for the bracketed photos.

Manual Focus: Exposures might vary somewhat when autofocus is used. Put your subject in manual focus and carefully adjust it to remove this danger.

RAW Power: Choose RAW file capture over JPEG. Because RAW files hold more tonal information, you may combine the bracketed exposures with more freedom in post-processing.

Recording the Bracketed Exposures:

Time to capture the moment with your camera set up and settings perfected! A few methods exist to start the bracketed exposures:

- **Remote Release**: Make an MC-DC2 or other similar investment. This removes the chance of camera shaking brought on by hitting the shutter button immediately.

- Press the shutter button gently if you don't have a remote release to reduce camera movement.

- **Use the self-timer on your camera**: Camera shaking is further reduced by allowing for a short wait before taking the picture.

Combining the Exposures in Brackets:

Your bracketed exposures are ready to be combined into a single HDR picture. Similar to "Merge to HDR Pro," most editing programs have specific HDR merging features. To get an amazing picture that accurately captures the dynamic range of the subject, combine the exposures as directed by the program, carefully balancing the highlights, midtones, and shadows.

Chapter Six
Utilizing Z8 Bracketing Features

More than just adjusting exposure for the ideal photo is bracketing. It enables you to investigate artistic options by taking a sequence of pictures with changes in white balance, exposure, or even Active D-Lighting (ADL). See it as using the finished picture to craft a "choose your own adventure" tale. Would you want a traditional well-exposed picture? Dramatic silhouette? Or maybe something with a distinctive color cast? Generally speaking, bracketing allows this.

Bracketing Powerhouse and The Z8:

With the Z8 you may investigate white balance and ADL fluctuations in addition to exposure. Photographers often employ Auto Exposure Bracketing (AEB) for important color accuracy. This records a series of photos, one at the "correct" exposure and then underexposed and overexposed photographs at predetermined intervals (often +3/-3 stops). Although AEB is the workhorse of color accuracy, the Z8 also has ADL bracketing for fine-tuning highlight and shadow detail, and white balance bracketing for recording the scene at various color temperatures.

The Potential of Bracketing:

Though first intimidating, configuring AEB on the Z8 is not as difficult as it seems. Below are the outlined explained simple steps:

Selecting Your Preferred Choice: Go into the "Auto Bracketing" area of the Photo Shooting menu. ADL bracketing, white balance bracketing, and even bracketing particular to flash are all available here; sort the brackets according to your artistic vision.

Telling Your Story: Your bracketed sequence may be ordered as you choose using Custom Setting e7. Is the "normal" exposure what you desire, then underexposed and overexposed photos? You get to decide that here.

Enter the Auto Bracketing option and choose "Number of Shots": This lets you choose how many photos—three, five, or whatever number you need to convey your visual narrative—you wish to take in the bracketed sequence.

The Fine-Tuning Touch: You may adjust the exposure difference between the images in the series by selecting "Increment". Select between more daring changes like 2 or 3 EV increments or more subdued ones like 1/3 or 2/3 EV increments. Recall that more photos may be in your bracketed collection at bigger intervals.

Finally, when everything is ready; just hit the shutter release button in Single-frame mode the predetermined number of times. Your selected bracketing software will determine how the Z8 automatically modifies exposure, white balance, or ADL to ensure you record a variety of options.

Note: Completing your bracketed sequence, turn off the bracketing feature by resetting the "Number of Shots" to zero. This guarantees that the bracketing function isn't inadvertently kept active.

Also, the Z8 has a streamlined bracketing method as well. With only one activation of the Bracketing Burst feature, every shutter release button push records a whole bracketed sequence, saving you time and effort. For even more flexibility, adjust the bracketing option using Custom Setting f2.

How to use the White Balance Bracketing

Especially for JPEG shooters, the Z8 makes white balance bracketing easier. The secret is in the fact that the camera initially captures only one RAW exposure when bracketing is turned on. Depending on your bracketing setup, it then produces excellent JPEG images with various white balance settings. Comparing this to taking many RAW photos, you may save time and storage space by having two or three JPEGs with the right degree of information with only one click.

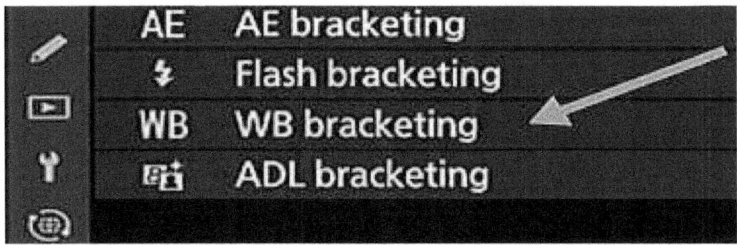

RAW versus JPEG Bracketing:

With all the data the sensor recorded, RAW files may seem to be the best option for bracketing. But by making JPEGs at various white balance settings, the Z8 simplifies the procedure. The camera's handling of RAW and JPEG in various shooting settings is broken out here:

JPEG-Only Mode: The camera discards the RAW data after the first RAW exposure is converted to a JPEG with your selected white balance settings. Efficiency is emphasized here.

RAW Mode: A Basic JPEG thumbnail is generated by the camera and included within the RAW (NEF) file. You see this thumbnail while looking through photos on the LCD screen. To modify the RAW file, open it in an image editing application.

Note: However, in RAW+JPEG Mode, the camera produces an additional JPEG file with the embedded thumbnail along with a separate JPEG file at your selected quality level (Fine, Normal, or Basic).

Fine-Tuning the Color Temperature:

Instead of modifying JPEG files by f-stops as exposure bracketing does, white balance bracketing modifies color temperature using micro reciprocal degrees, or mirrors. The amber-blue spectrum is notably affected by a 5-mired color temperature change applied to each picture in the bracketed collection, leaving the green-magenta balance unaffected. This lets you adjust your picture's general warmth or coldness.

Turning on White Balance Bracketing:

Image Quality Configuration: Go to the Photo Shooting menu and make sure "JPEG-Only" is checked under the "Image Quality" section.

Bracketing Configuration: Find the "Auto Bracketing" option under Photo Shooting. Here's where you choose "WB Bracketing" as your bracketing setup.

Shots: Go to the "Number of Shots" area after choosing WB Bracketing. Here you have two choices:

Balanced Shots: Select between zero and nine shots using the right directional button. This guarantees a proportionate distribution of pictures on the two extremes of the white balance range. Five photos, for instance, would provide one neutral image and two each with a bias of five and 10 mireds in the amber and blue directions, respectively.

Directional biases: To choose two or three photos with either blue (B) or amber (A) biases, use the left directional button. To investigate colder color temperatures, choose "B3," for example, to get three pictures with blue biases of 5, 10, and 15 mireds.

Lastly, to guarantee your photos always include the most realistic and attractive colors, experiment, investigate several color variants, and capture the ideal mood and atmosphere in your subject.

How to use the ADL Bracketing

ADL bracketing enhances the power of ADL, Nikon's innovative technology for preserving detail in highlights and shadows, to a whole new level. Enabling ADL bracketing allows you to capture a series of images with different ADL settings. With this feature, you can apply various interpretations of the scene's lighting and select the one that aligns perfectly with your photographic desire.

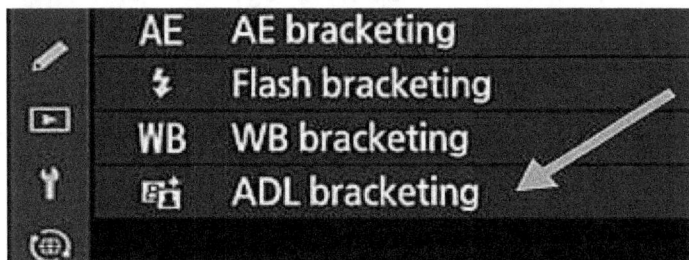

Mastering the Settings:

To activate ADL bracketing, you can find the "Auto Bracketing Set" option in the Photo Shooting menu. Welcome to your mission control center for configuring the bracketing behavior. Here is a detailed analysis of the available options:

Zero Shots: Disabling ADL bracketing will result in zero shots. On the other hand, if ADL is enabled within the Shooting menu, the basic ADL settings (Auto to Low) could still be applied to individual images.

Two Shots: This feature allows you to capture two images for comparison purposes. The first image is taken with ADL deactivated, serving as a control, while the second image is taken with your selected ADL setting. Use the "Amount" box to easily switch between different options for ADL processing, allowing you to customize the level of processing as needed.

3-5 Shots: This feature provides increased flexibility as it allows you to capture three, four, or five images in the bracket sequence. When capturing images, it's important to keep in mind that one image will always serve as a reference with ADL deactivated, while the rest will be taken with different ADL settings. Here is a detailed analysis:

3 Shots: Capture pictures with ADL set to Low, Normal, and Off.

4 Shots: Allows you to capture images with different ADL settings: Off, Low, Normal, and High.

5 Shots: Allows you to capture images with different ADL settings: Off, Low, Normal, High, and Extra High.

Ensuring a Uniform Approach:

Just like with other bracketing modes on the Z8, it's important to remember to disable ADL bracketing when it's not being used. Unlike exposure bracketing, ADL bracketing remains active until it is manually turned off, providing a convenient and reliable feature for photographers. This guarantees reliable outcomes and avoids any unforeseen ADL processing on your images. Disabling it can be done using the same procedure as exposure or white balance bracketing.

Recommendations:

The Z8 also provides a streamlined approach to ADL bracketing. If you have a good understanding of camera settings, you may have a designated "Bracketing Burst" button that allows you to capture a burst of images with different ADL settings based on your bracketing configuration. This simplifies the process and helps you save valuable time.

Chapter Seven
The Flash

Electronic Flash

Many professional photographers now utilize electronic studio lighting because it freezes activity and is more intense (which the photographer may alter using the strobe's power adjustment options). Unless you wish to utilize a tripod to lock down a composition, flash offers a fast, constant light quality that mimics sunshine. (Although color balance varies as flash duration decreases, some Nikon flash units can transmit the precise white balance selected for that photo.) Even experts will concede that an external flash has useful uses as an adjunct, especially to fill in shadows or act as a wireless trigger for more off-camera strobes. It is not necessary to utilize it in direct-flash mode.

However, using electrical flash is not as simple as using continuous illumination. Although they are more expensive, electronic flash devices do not provide a precise preview of the lighting effect (unless you add a second source or mode known as a modeling light).

When an electrical charge builds up in a component known as a capacitor, photons are created and sent through a glass tube filled with xenon gas, which absorbs the energy and releases the light burst. When in automated mode (known by Nikon **as iTTL**), the primary flash is preceded by one or more mini-bursts, known as "**monitor preflash**," which enable wireless communication with other external flash units connected and measurement of the amount of light reflecting off your subject and backdrop. External strobes may be connected to the camera in some ways:

Camera-mounted/hardwired external dedicated flash: Nikon or other manufacturers' units that work with the Creative Lighting System (CLS) may be connected via a wired system like the Nikon SC-28/SC-29 cables or hooked into the accessory "hot" shoe.

Wireless dedicated flash: Signals generated during a pre-flash (before the main flash burst) may activate a CLS-compatible flash unit and provide two-way communication between the camera and flash unit. A wireless non-flashing accessory, like the Nikon SU-800, which just "talks" to the external flashes, or a CLS-compatible flash unit in Master mode may both serve as the triggering flash.

Wired, non-intelligent mode: The Z8 comes with an integrated dedicated old-style PC/X connection; if not, you can simply install one by slipping the Nikon AS-15 Sync Terminal converter into the hot shoe. One piece of data, one way, is sent via the PC/X connection, a non-intelligent camera/flash link: it instructs a linked flash to ignite. Nothing more is exchanged between the flash and the camera. Non-dedicated/non-CLS-friendly strobes may be connected via the PC/X connection. These can include manual non-CLS flash, studio flash units, flash units from other vendors that can utilize a PC cable or even Nikon-brand speedlights that you choose to connect in a non-CLS, "unintelligent" mode.

Radio/Infrared transmitter/receivers: Using an add-on wireless infrared or radio transmitter like the Nikon WR-R11a/WR-T10, PocketWizard, Radio Popper, a Paul C. Buff CyberSync trigger, or the Godox device, or a dedicated radio-compatible flash unit like the Nikon SB-5000, is another way to connect flash units to the camera. Typically installed on the accessory shoe, they indicate when the camera gives the order to fire via the hot shoe. The most basic of these only serves as a wireless PC/X connection; the flash and camera communicate only when the flash is told to fire. Sophisticated models, however, have their internal controllers and, when linked to suitable flash units, may transmit extra orders to the receivers.

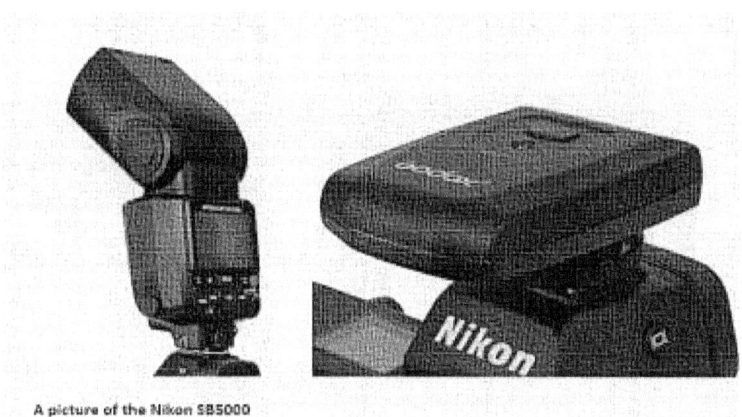

A picture of the Nikon SB5000

Easy optical connection: The most popular method, though it has become obsolete, to activate off-camera, non-wired flash units in the days before clever wireless communication was via something known as a slave unit. Small external triggers linked to the remote flash or integrated within the flash itself, these remote units activate when the optical sensor detects a burst started by a flash attached to the camera. It triggers the off-camera flash units fast enough to contribute to the same exposure when it "sees" the main flash. Apart from the absence of any intelligent communication between the camera and flash, the primary issue with this kind of connection is that any pre-flashes released by the other strobes may confuse the receiver unit and cause it to fire too soon. Special "digital" modes on modern triggers fire exclusively from the main flash burst, ignoring the preflash.

Selecting a Flash Synch Mode

There are five flash sync modes on the Z8 and a sixth (High-Speed Sync, covered later) that are activated under certain conditions. The Flash Mode option (Z8) in the Photo Shooting menu allows selection of the five primary modes as well as

Off, which turns off the flash. Those modes are listed below:

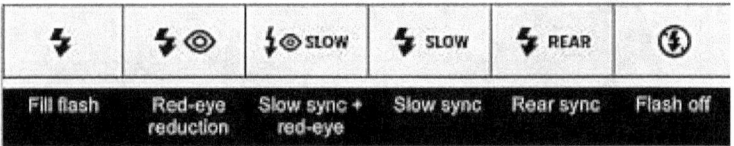

Fill flash/Front-curtain sync: This should be your default option; it is available in Auto and PSAM modes. The electronic front curtain unfolds fully in this mode, at which point the flash goes off. Once the exposure is over, the electronic shutter stays open until the electronic rear curtain shuts. Movement will result in the secondary "ghost" exposure that appears in front of the flash exposure if the subject is moving and the ambient light levels are high enough.

Rear-curtain sync (available in PSAM modes): The front curtain fully opens and stays open throughout the exposure when the rear curtain is synced with Program, Shutter-priority, Aperture-priority, or Manual exposure modes. The electrical back curtain shuts and the flash is then discharged. Moving subjects will produce a secondary "ghost" exposure that appears behind (trailing) the flash exposure if the ambient light levels are high enough. What follows is more on "ghost" exposures. This option instructs the camera, in Program and Aperture-priority modes, to balance ambient light with flash illumination by combining rear-curtain sync with slow shutter rates.

Red-eye reduction (available in Auto and PSAM modes): This mode reduces possible red-eye effects by using the red-eye reduction function of the attached flash unit to cause the subject's pupils to contract (assuming they are looking at the camera) during the one-second lag after pressing the shutter release before the picture is taken. Just before the primary flash burst for exposure, the SB-5000 and SB-500 speedlights release three brief flash bursts. The green AF-illuminator light on the camera briefly glows before the main burst is triggered by other Nikon flash units. Use red-eye reduction sparingly and only when you can stand the wait.

Slow sync (available in P or A modes): This option enables Program and Aperture-priority modes to employ shutter speeds as slow as 30 seconds with the flash to help balance your primary subject, which will be lit by the electronic flash, with a backdrop lit with ambient light. Naturally, slower shutter speeds will be best achieved using a tripod.

Slow Sync + Red Eye: When utilizing Program or Aperture-priority settings, this mode—which is accessible in Auto and PA modes—combines slow sync with the red-eye mitigation feature of the external flash.

Flash off: The flash does not fire even when it is turned on (available in Auto and PSAM modes).

Ghost Images

If ambient light in your environment also affects the picture, the choice between front-curtain sync (the default setting) and rear-curtain sync (an optional parameter) may make a big impact. Faster shutter speeds—1/200th second in particular—don't give the ambient light much time to register unless it's very bright. Since the electronic flash will probably provide almost all of the light, front- or rear-curtain sync is not necessary.

There is a big difference, however, especially if your subject is moving or the camera isn't stable, at shorter shutter speeds or with very intense ambient light levels. Wherever there is movement (camera or subject), the ambient light will register as a second picture that is not in the same location as the flash exposure. It will appear as a ghost image and, if the movement is strong enough, as a hazy ghost image trailing in the direction of the movement in front of or behind your subject.

With front-curtain sync, the subject is captured on the sensor and the flash turns off as soon as the shutter opens. Then the electronic shutter stays open for a further time (between 30 and 1/200th seconds). The ambient light ghost picture will cause a blur on the right side of the original subject image if your subject is moving, say, toward the right side of the frame.

Rear-curtain sync is thus offered by Nikon to address the problem; this setting opens the electronic shutter just as it did previously. The ghost picture develops while the shutter stays open for the allotted time. The ghost will move from left to right as well if your subject goes from the left side of the frame to the right. Then, 1.3 milliseconds before the back shutter curtain shuts, the flash is fired, creating a lovely, crisp flash picture ahead of the ghost image.

Handling Sync Speed Issues

Over 1/200th second shutter speeds might be problematic. Thinking about it, it makes perfect logic to trigger the electrical flash only when the virtual shutter is fully open. Only a portion of the sensor is exposed at a time to achieve shutter rates quicker than 1/200th second, by beginning the second curtain to "descend" before the first curtain has fully opened. With a shutter slit across the sensor's surface, that essentially gives a shorter exposure. The only aperture that would be seen if the flash fired while the front and back curtains were partly covering the sensor would be the open one.

Just a narrow band would remain, signifying the area of the sensor that was visible at the time the photo was taken. The rear curtains move before the front curtains reach the bottom of the picture with shutter speeds quicker than 1/200th second. Thus, as it descends from the top to the bottom, a moving slit—the space between the front and back curtains—exposes a section of the sensor at a time.

Just the exposed part of the sensor will be illuminated if the flash is set off while this slit is moving. The back electronic curtain, which had begun to "move" when the flash was activated, is what is concealed by the black band at the bottom of the picture. Readers with keen eyes will ask why the back curtain starts its trip at the top of the frame, not the bottom. The explanation is easy: your lens produces the picture on the sensor in a reversed orientation by turning it upside down. The camera is clever enough to display the pixels that comprise your image in the correct orientation during picture evaluation, so you never realize that. But this picture flip is the reason why, while manually cleaning a sensor, you should search for the speck in the bottom half of the sensor if you see a bit of dust in the top half of a test shot.

Except in the studio, utilizing studio flash units instead of my Nikon-dedicated Speedlights, might you run into sync-speed issues. That's because, with a "smart" flash (such as one of the Nikon Speedlights), any inadvertent shutter speed settings are rectified when a strobe is added. Should you choose to set the shutter speed to a faster speed in S or M mode and are not using High-Speed Sync, the flash will instantly change the shutter speed to 1/200th second (or prevent you from selecting a higher speed if the flash is already turned up). When utilizing flash, in A or P modes when the camera chooses the shutter speed, it will never pick a shutter speed faster than 1/200th second. Flashing in P mode automatically sets the shutter speed from 1/60th to 1/200th second.

But the camera has no means of detecting that a flash is attached when using a non-dedicated flash, like a studio unit linked into an adapter fitted on the accessory shoe, therefore shutter rates quicker than 1/200th second might be set mistakenly. You can use the manual exposure and the 1/200th-second shutter speed (or slower, as certain studio flash units may demand) to prevent that issue with studio flash.

High-Speed Sync

Keep in mind that the Z8 has a feature called "high-speed sync" that lets you use some external Nikon flash units with shutter speeds faster than 1/200th second. When Auto FP high-speed sync is used, the flash fires some bursts at lower power for the whole exposure. This lets the light reach the sensor even as the slit moves. The settings that change the suitable external flash are used to set high-speed sync (HSS); there's no extra setting you need to do on the flash.

Hence, it makes a lot of sense to only use the electric flash when the shutter is fully open. To get shutter speeds faster than 1/200th second, the back curtain is opened before the front curtain is fully open. This means that only part of the sensor is visible at a time. Because a hole in the shutter moves over the sensor's surface, that gives the picture a shorter exposure. If the flash went off while the front and back curtains partially blocked the sensor, only the area bounded by the open slit would be seen.

When shooting outdoors, this method works best when you need a fill-in flash but 1/200th second is too slow for the f/stop you want to use. Outside, an exposure at ISO 200 is likely to be 1/200th second at, say, f/14, which is fine for an ambient/balanced fill-flash exposure if you don't mind the very shallow depth of field that the small f/stop gives you. What if you'd rather shoot at f/5.6 for 1/1600th of a second? This is possible with high-speed sync, and the lower flash power shouldn't bother you since you're after the fill-flash anyway. This sync mode gives you more options than, say, switching to ISO 100.

High-speed sync is also helpful when you want to use a bigger f/stop to narrow the depth of field for selective focus. If you choose a shutter speed faster than 1/200th second, the faster sync speed will lower the flash's useful light without you having to do anything else.

Auto FP high-speed sync can be used with the Nikon SB-5000, SB-910/SB-900, SB-700, SB-500, SB-R200, and some older Speedlights like the SB-800 and SB-600. There is no setting on the flash itself that needs to be changed. Setting e1 must be used to choose 1/200 s (Auto FP) or 1/250th s (Auto FP). If you connect an external flash that works with the camera and use the P or A exposure modes, the shutter speed will be set to 1/200th to 1/250th second. Then, shutter speeds faster than 1/200th to 1/250th second, all the way up to 1/8000th second, can be used with full sync, though the flash power will be less. Setting the flash sync speed to less than 1/200th second might also be a good idea sometimes, like when you want the background light to create extra ghost pictures in the picture. You can select from the following options:

1/200s (Auto FP) 1/250ths (Auto FP): These settings let you use compatible external flash units with high-speed synchronization at 1/200th or 1/250th second or faster. They also turn on Auto FP sync when the camera chooses a shutter speed of 1/200th to 1/250th second or faster in Programmed and Aperture-priority modes. Other flash units will only be used at speeds of 1/200th of a second or less.

1/200s: When this setting is used, flash can only be used with shutter speeds up to 1/200th second. This is what you'd use with "dumb" studio flash units.

1/200s-1/60s: The shutter speed ranges from 1/200th second to 1/60th second. You can choose a particular shutter speed from this range to be used as the timing speed for external flash units. A "slow-sync" effect happens when you force the picture speed to be slower. When 1/60th second is set as the fastest flash shutter speed, for example, light from the room is more likely to affect the exposure. That can help balance the flash intensity with the light that's already hitting the background. When you want to make it look like something is moving, that slow picture speed can create ghost images. Other times, it can be done by accident. To cut down on ghost pictures, you might need to use a tripod or VR.

How to Use External Flash

This part talks about the Nikon Creative Lighting System (CLS). It was first shown off in July 2003, when the company released the SB-800 Speedlight, a flash unit that worked with early professional digital SLRs like the Nikon D2h/D2hs and, a few months later, cheaper models like the Nikon D70 and all the company's other digital cameras. The following are some of CLS's features, though not all of them work with all Nikon cameras:

i-TTL: Smart through-the-lens exposure control figures out exposure based on a monitor pre-flash that fires a fraction of a second before the main burst. The exposure is then judged by the same RGB exposure sensor that measures continuous light. Because the system is smart, it can make complex changes, like combining the flash exposure with the natural light exposure when you're shooting in broad daylight to fill in the blacks.

Advanced wireless lighting (AWL): This is a system that uses the same preflash idea to send triggers and exposure information to external flash units that aren't directly connected to the camera but are close by (about 30 feet). You might be able to separate up to three flash units into different "groups" and talk to them using any of four "channels." This way, you can keep your flash units from being activated by another Nikon photographer's master flash nearby.

FV Lock: A flash value locking method lets you keep the current flash exposure. This way, you can measure flash exposure for a topic that isn't in the middle of the frame, then resize and use that value for future exposures. It is possible to set up a Fn button to do this. When the flash is attached to the hot shoe and the FV lock is turned on, the camera only measures the middle part of the frame, even if Matrix metering is chosen. In wireless modes, the average of the whole frame is used for measuring.

Automatic FP high-speed sync: Focal plane HS sync lets you sync an external flash when the shutter speed is faster than 1/200th second. If the flash and camera are compatible, shutter speeds of up to 1/8000th second can be used.

However, only a small portion of the flash's light is used, and the flash's range is limited, sometimes to just a few feet.

Focus assist: There is built-in lighting for focus assist, but the CLS system also lets wide-area AF-assist lighting be added to the front of the flash unit or to a line that connects the flash to the camera. Extra focus helps to let you see farther away or across a larger area.

Zoom Coverage: Some CLS-compatible flash units come with a controlled zoom head that lets you change the flash's coverage area to match the lens's focal length, which is sent from the camera to the flash. You can also zoom in and out by hand.

Flash Color Information Communication: If you change the length of the flash burst, the light from a CLS-compatible flash can have a different color temperature. At first, the flash is mostly blue, but as the burst goes on, it turns redder. If you want to change the white balance in AWB mode, the Speedlight can send information to the camera about the flash's true color information.

How to Use Flash Exposure Compensation

If you don't like the exposure your flash gives you, you can add or take away exposure from the flash exposure that the camera figures out. You can use the Flash Compensation option in the Photo Shooting menu or Custom Setting f2: Custom Controls to link Flash Mode/Flash Compensation to a button, like Fn1. When a command dial is given to a button, you can change Flash Mode by pressing and turning the main command dial. To change Flash Compensation, hold down the button and turn the sub-command dial. From -3 EV to +1 EV, you can make changes in 1/3 EV steps.

As with regular exposure compensation, the change you make stays in place until you "zero" it out. To do this, press the button for flash mode/flash compensation and turn the subcommand wheel until it shows "0" on the monochrome control panel and the screen. Press the button to see the current setting for flash exposure correction. An icon will show up on the screen when compensation is being used.

Further, **Custom Setting e3: Exposure Compensation** for Flash lets you balance flash exposure and background light across the whole frame, or it can only be used for the background. This choice tells the camera how to change the flash level when exposure adjustment is used. It has different settings for natural light exposure compensation and flash exposure compensation. If you are using Flash, you can change either one or both of them. When you use Flash along with Custom Setting e3, it only changes the atmospheric exposure correction. It controls how atmospheric exposure adjustment is used when a flash unit is also used to add to the light:

Entire frame: To change the ambient exposure compensation, press the EV button on the top panel, which is to the right of the ISO button, and turn the main command dial. This changes both the ambient and flash exposure compensation for the whole frame. That gives both parts the same amount of contact.

Just the background: When this choice is chosen, only atmospheric exposure compensation changes when you use it. Flash exposure compensation stays the same. So, exposure correction only affects the parts of your picture that are in the background and are usually lit by natural light. Flash exposure compensation is not changed, but it can be set separately if you've used Custom Setting f2 to link Flash Mode/Compensation to a button, as we already talked about. If so, all you have to do to change the flash correction is turn the sub-command dial.

Chapter Eight

Understanding and Using the Exposure Modes on the Z8

It's not just about the settings; exposure is a discussion with light itself. The first thing you notice is the master, which is the main source of light, like the sun's golden touch or a lamp's soft glow. Then you follow its path, seeing how it reacts with your subject, hits things, or shows you things you didn't know. The light turns into your language, and contact turns into the tool you use to translate it.

The Three Instruments: ISO, Aperture, and Shutter Speed:

You can control this dance with three tools from the Z-series: aperture, shutter speed, and ISO. Think of the aperture as the camera's eye, which controls how much light gets in. A bigger aperture lets in more light, while a smaller aperture makes the depth of field shorter, which makes your subject stand out in a sea of mush.

Shutter speed, on the other hand, tells you how long the light works on the camera. A faster speed stops moving things in their tracks, while a slower speed makes a dreamy blur that's great for catching lights or water falling.

ISO is a measure of how sensitive the sensor is to light. It's kind of like turning up the sound. A higher ISO speeds up the sensor's reaction, which is great when there isn't much light, but it can also add noise that you don't want, like static in a song.

Keeping the Light in Check:

There is no performer among these instruments; they all play together. When it's bright, increasing the lens size lets you use a faster shutter speed or a lower ISO. If there isn't much light, on the other hand, you may need a bigger lens, a slower shutter speed, or a higher ISO. To master exposure, you need to understand these connections and find the right mix to get the result you want.

Expressing Yourself Through Exposure:

A well-exposed picture shows the scene in all its beauty. On the other hand, purposely underexposing can make the picture mysterious, and slightly overexposing can make it look like a dream. When you expose something, light and shade become your paintbrush, and you use them to make a picture.

Looking at the Differences: Further Analysis:

Let's look into each instrument in more detail:

Lighting Strength: Figuring out the strength of the light source, whether it's natural or manmade, lets you change the exposure to fit. You can fine-tune the light's song by spreading out harsh sunlight or changing the flash power.

Light Length: Not all sources of light stay on all the time. If you want to get the best picture of a flash or a burst of motion, you have to change the shutter speed.

Light Interaction: There are interesting ways that light can affect your subject. By changing the amount and quality of light that reaches your subject, you can change the exposure by knowing how it reflects, transmits, or emits light.

Mastering F-stops and Shutter Speeds

Consider the human eye, a biological engineering wonder that changes to collect the constantly shifting light of the environment. The goal of your Z-series camera is comparable even if it doesn't have a beating heart. How then does it communicate in light's language? Here is when the dynamic pair of your camera for exposure control, aperture, and shutter speed, come into play.

F-Stops:

Consider the aperture to be your camera's iris—a gateway that controls how much light can get in. Written as f/ followed by a number, it functions as a ratio; a lower value indicates a wider aperture, allowing in a flood of light, while a bigger number produces a narrower aperture, similar to a squinting eye. Still, the shift isn't straightforward. Every whole f-stop jump corresponds to a half or doubling of light transmission. Moving from f/4 to f/2, therefore, lets in twice as much light, which is ideal for catching quick moments in dimly lit settings. Be advised, however, that a larger aperture also changes the depth of field—the region that is in focus. A shallower depth of focus produced by a larger aperture blurs the backdrop and isolates your subject in a dreamy haze.

The Shutter Speed:

Shutter speed determines how long light stays on the camera's sensor while aperture governs how much of it there is. Consider a waterfall; for movement photography, a slow shutter speed lets the water elude into a smooth cascade. Fast shutter speeds, on the other hand, stop activity in its tracks and are ideal for catching a youngster laughing or a bird in mid-flight. Usually stated as fractions of a second, shutter speeds are 1/60th, 1/125th, 1/250th, and 1/500th. Quotation marks are used by your reliable Z-series to prevent misunderstanding for longer exposures; figures like 2", 2.5", and 4" indicate exposures lasting a cool 2, 2.5, and 4 seconds. At night, these slower speeds enable you to photograph the enchantment of light trails from moving stars or the seamless flow of cars.

Combining the Two:

Recall that shutter speed and aperture go hand in together. Lower light conditions let you utilize a quicker shutter speed by increasing the aperture. Conversely, a slower shutter speed is required with a smaller aperture. Understanding this complex dance—balancing the length and quantity of light to get the desired effect—is the key to mastering exposure. Expressing your perspective is more important than only details. While a purposeful underexposure may provide drama and a little overexposure can conjure a dreamy aspect, a well-exposed picture highlights the intricacies of the scene.

Achieving Equivalent Exposure

Aperture Versus Shutter Speed (Striking a Balance):

See aperture to be the size of your eye's pupil; a larger opening allows more light in, whilst a smaller one limits it. This has a direct influence on depth of field, or how much of your picture seems crisp. A bigger aperture results in a shallow depth of focus, which is great for isolating your subject against a dreamy blur in the backdrop. In contrast, a smaller aperture maintains everything crisp from foreground to background.

In contrast, shutter speed determines how long the camera's sensor is exposed to light. A quicker shutter speed stops activity in its tracks, ideal for photographing a bird in flight. But it also allows for less light. In contrast, a slower shutter speed enables more light to penetrate, which is good for low-light circumstances, but it might blur moving objects.

Applying the ISO Sensitivity:

ISO sensitivity functions like a volume knob on your camera's sensor. Increasing the ISO makes it more sensitive to light, which is advantageous in low-light circumstances. However, it may contribute to unnecessary noise, resulting in a grainy picture.

Equivalence: Ensuring Consistent Exposure:

The beauty in the notion of equal exposure is the total quantity of light hitting the sensor stays consistent regardless of the aperture and shutter speed settings. You can get the same exposure with a wide aperture and a quick shutter speed, or a small aperture and a slow shutter speed. This technique enables you to keep constant exposure while experimenting with depth of field and motion blur artistically.

Simplifying the Process: Program Mode:

For individuals new to photography, your Z-series camera has a Program (P) option. The camera's brain takes the wheel, automatically determining the best aperture and shutter speed combination for optimum exposure.

Unlocking Creative Control: Flexible Program:

But what if you want greater control? Enter the Flexible Program, represented by a "P*" on your camera. This mode enables you to change the aperture and shutter speed combination (equivalent exposure) via the command dial while the camera maintains the overall exposure level. This allows you to experiment with various creative effects, such as blurring motion or isolating your subject, all within the ease of Program mode.

Calculating Exposure Correctly

The Value of Gray and Focus:

Accurate exposure depends heavily on focus. From what is in focus, the camera assumes something about the scene. Its goal is to make everything a neutral medium gray, usually around 18% gray. Cameras, however, may prefer a tint closer to black since they are tuned somewhat differently than human vision.

Highlighting the Center: Assumptions and Metering:

The camera meters certain regions within the targeted area to ascertain exposure. These regions should reflect light around 12–18% gray, or like a medium gray card. The reason this assumption is important is that various things reflect light differently. If the camera is focusing on the black cat, our white cat may be in the spotlight and be washed out in the finished picture.

Analyzing Exposure: Striking the Correct Notes:

Realism in tones and detail needs precise exposure. Ideally, the camera meter would recognize light reflected from a middle-gray region and change the exposure to properly capture it in the picture. In the finished image, this means that the black and white patches seem realistic.

Interpretation: Overexposure and Underexposure:

When the camera misreads a dark region for the intended middle gray, overexposure results. It raises exposure to make darker regions seem grayer. On the other hand, underexposure results from a camera trying to make a bright region seem mid-gray, which reduces exposure and produces dark, muddy shadows.

Handling the Light: Reaching Ideal Exposure:

Photographers typically utilize a gray card, a dependable source of constant light reflection, for exact exposure control. The two main components of exposure, aperture and shutter speed, are also controlled to varying degrees by different shooting modes; some popular choices are Aperture-priority, Shutter-priority, Program, and Manual. In the end, a great photo balances acceptable noise levels, motion blur, and desirable depth-of-field in the finished picture.

Analyzing the Various Exposure Types

Aperture Priority (A)

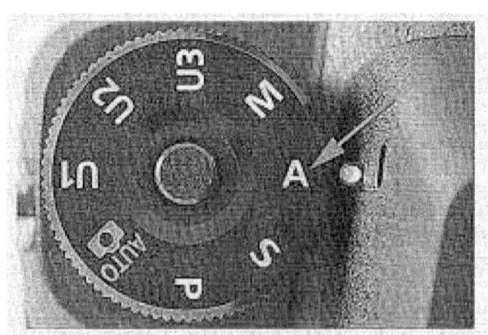

- Set the aperture (f-stop) and the shutter speed to get the right exposure. This mode is great for controlling depth of field, or the blur behind your image.
- Use big apertures (low f-numbers) for backgrounds that are fuzzy and small apertures (high f-numbers) for scenes that are clear.

Shutter Priority (S)

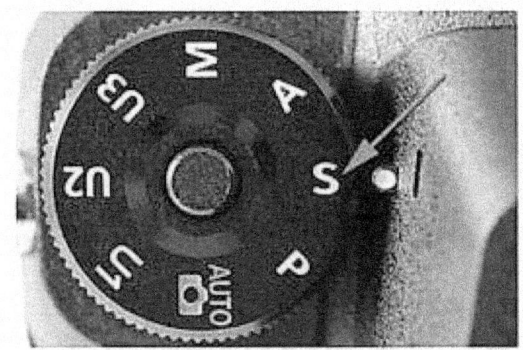

- Great for capturing blurred movements or stopping activity.
- You pick the shutter speed, and the camera changes the aperture to get the right picture.
- You can freeze movement with fast shutter speeds and add artistic motion blur with slow shutter speeds

Program Mode (P)

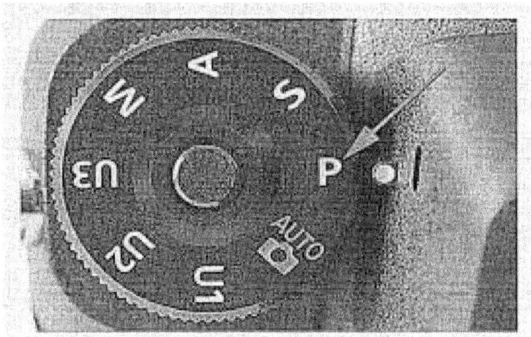

- The camera sets the aperture and shutter speed automatically so that the picture is well-lit. This mode is great for beginners or quick shots where you don't need to be very exact.
- Gives you some freedom to change the exposure.

Manual Mode (M)

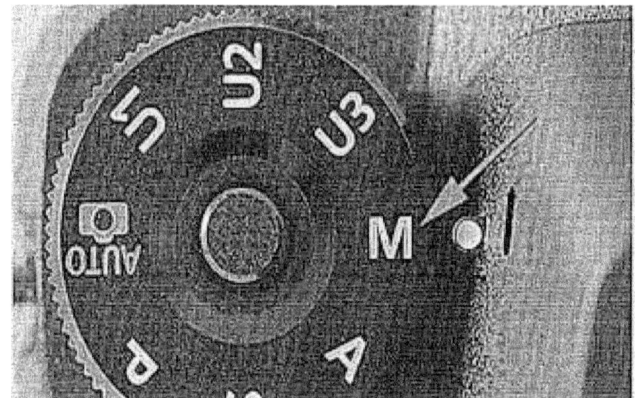

- Gives you full control over the aperture, shutter speed, and ISO. It's great for studio photography, flash photography, and situations with tricky lighting.
- You have to put in the exposure you want to get the results you want.

Tips for Picking the Right Mode:

- Use aperture priority to change the depth of the field in creative ways.
- Shutter Priority to record moving or still objects.
- Program Mode for quick shots and ease of use.
- Manual Mode gives you full power and lets you be creative.

Leveraging ISO Settings for Exposure Adjustment

Mastering ISO vis-à-vis the Light-Gathering:

ISO technically describes the light sensitivity of your camera. It modifies how much light the sensor collects, much like a light-gathering ninja. Bright surroundings are best served by lower ISO settings (such as ISO 100), whereas low-light conditions are better served by higher ISO settings (such as ISO 6400).

Mastering Creative Control with ISO:

ISO is something many photographers set and forget. The trick, however, is that ISO is a potent instrument for adjusting exposure (brightness) in different photography settings. Examine its possibilities now:

The Manual Mode: You have total control over ISO, shutter speed, and aperture while using manual mode. Fine-tuning exposure using ISO enables you to get your desired brightness even with a certain aperture or shutter speed.

In the Program, Aperture-priority, and Shutter-priority modes: They all gain from ISO modification, for instance, assuming you would like a sharper picture in aperture-priority mode, so you set the shutter speed quicker. That quicker shutter speed may be maintained without sacrificing exposure by increasing ISO.

Tracking Down the ISO Sweet Spot:

There is a trade-off even if higher ISO settings let you shoot in dim lighting. Image quality may suffer when you increase the ISO because unwelcome noise, or grain, might seep into your photos. While noise is greatly reduced at higher ISOs by modern cameras like the z8, finding the ideal balance between desired brightness and tolerable noise is still crucial.

ISO Powerhouse and the z8:

With a startling Lo 1 (equal to ISO 32) for very bright conditions and an astounding Hi 2 (equivalent to ISO 204,800) for near-darkness photography, the z8 offers an amazing ISO range. This wide range enables you to take amazing pictures in any kind of illumination.

Auto ISO:

Auto ISO may be a lifesaver; it will automatically change sensitivity to keep shutter speeds at their optimal and reduce blur. Limits must be established, nevertheless, to avoid the camera choosing too high ISOs that might produce undesired noise.

Chapter Nine
Movie Shooting

Basic Movie Recording Operation

Getting Ready to Record:

1. **Touch the camera screen** to initiate the movie recording.
2. The screen displays the remaining recording time and the frame area being captured.

Starting and Stopping Recording:

1. Press the dedicated **movie-record button** to begin recording. Recording starts with the camera power-on and focuses on the center of the frame.
2. Use the **Pause/Play button** to temporarily stop and resume recording. Recording automatically stops after five minutes of pause (except in HS movie mode).
3. Press the **"end" button** to permanently stop recording.

Playback:

1. Switch to full-frame viewing mode for movie selection and playback.
2. Locate movies using the **movie options icon**.

Focusing During Recording:

The autofocus mode (set in the movie menu) determines focus behavior:

- **Single AF:** Focus locks at recording start. Use the multi-selector to refocus during recording.
- **Full-time AF:** Focus continuously adjusts while recording. Note: The AE/AF Lock button might

function differently. Press the button to lock focus during recording, and press again to unlock.

Manual Focus:

Rotate the side dial while recording in manual focus mode to adjust the focus manually.

Exposure Control:

The exposure lock setting (in the setup menu) determines exposure behavior during recording:

- **AE/AF Lock, AE Lock Only, or AE Lock (Hold):** Press the AE/AF lock button to lock exposure while recording. Press again to unlock.

- **[AF Lock Only]:** Use the multi-selector to lock brightness during recording. Press the AE/AF lock button again to unlock.

Maximum Recording Time:

- The camera screen displays the remaining recording time for a single movie.

- Each movie file is limited to a maximum of 29 minutes or 4GB, regardless of available memory card space. Larger files are automatically split for playback continuity.

- High camera temperatures may shorten recording times.

- Actual recording time can vary depending on the movie content, subject movement, and memory card type.

Memory Card Recommendations:

- Use SD cards with an SD Speed Class rating of 6 (Video Speed Class V6) or faster for optimal movie recording.

- For recording in [2160/30p] or [2160/25p] (4K UHD) codecs, use UHS Speed Class 3 (Video Speed Class V30) or faster cards. Slower cards may cause unexpected recording interruptions.

Camera Temperature Notes:
- The camera may overheat during prolonged movie recording in hot environments.
- Recording automatically stops if the camera reaches a critical temperature. A timer displays the remaining time before the recording stops. The camera powers off upon recording completion.
- Allow the camera to cool down sufficiently before resuming operation after overheating.

Recording Movie Notes:
- While saving movies, the camera may display flashing lights or a "Please wait" message. To prevent data loss or camera/card damage, avoid opening the battery compartment/card slot or removing the battery/card during this time.

Recorded Movie Characteristics:
- Recorded movies may capture various operational sounds, including zoom adjustments, side dial operations, autofocus lens movements, vibration reduction activity, and automatic aperture changes in response to lighting conditions.
- Some lighting scenarios (fluorescent, mercury-vapor, sodium-vapor) may introduce banding effects in recorded footage.
- Fast-moving objects (trains, cars) may appear distorted in recordings.
- Rapid panning movements can cause the entire movie frame to appear skewed.

- Bright areas may leave residual trails on the screen during camera movement.
- Moiré patterns (colored lines) may appear on subjects with repeating patterns (fabrics, windows) due to interactions between the subject and the camera's sensor structure. This is not a malfunction.

Autofocus Considerations:

Autofocus might struggle in certain scenarios with poorly defined subjects. Here are some tips:

- Choose Single AF (default) or another suitable autofocus mode from the movie menu before recording.
- If autofocus encounters difficulties, temporarily shift focus to a different subject within the frame at a similar distance. Start recording and then adjust framing as needed.

Types of Video Files

You may capture videos in a range of formats with the Nikon Z8 to match your computer capabilities and editing requirements. Below are the options:

For professional raw editing:

Professional editors using powerful machines will find N-RAW 12-bit (NEV) to be perfect. For flexibility in post-production, this format records raw, unprocessed video data. It cannot, however, be played back on most devices and editing calls on relatively strong computers. A lesser, 1920 x 1080 H.264 proxy video (MP4) is also recorded by the camera for internal viewing. You may change the video quality settings and choose from two color profiles (SDR and N-Log). There is an excellent PCM recording of the audio.

File types like N-RAW, and ProRes RAW HQ 12-bit (MOV) are intended for expert RAW editing. For example, using the ProRes RAW format provides the same raw video data for ultimate control while maybe providing various editing program compatibility. It supports SDR and N-Log color profiles and comes with a proxy video for playback, much like N-RAW. There is a PCM recording of the audio.

For Improved Editing:

Options under here include: **ProRes 422 HQ 10-bit (MOV):** This format puts file size last. Maintaining reasonable file sizes, it employs a high-bitrate codec (ProRes 422 HQ) appropriate for expert editing and color grading.

Recording audio in PCM format: This provides SDR and N-Log color profiles.

For Compression and Quality:

H.265 10-bit (MOV): This format strikes a nice compromise between file size and picture quality. Good color detail is achieved by using the effective 10-bit color depth H.265 codec. Recording audio in PCM format supports three color profiles (SDR, HLG, and N-Log).

For Smaller File Sizes:

H.265 8-bit (MOV): This format gives greater compression of file precedence. For online sharing or less taxing editing tasks, it makes use of the 8-bit color depth H.265 codec. It captures sound in PCM format and only provides an SDR color profile.

H.264 8-bit (MP4): This provides tiny file sizes and excellent interoperability. It is appropriate for minimal editing or online sharing and utilizes the H.264 codec with 8-bit color depth. AAC format audio is captured for greater interoperability.

Types of Tone Modes

The Nikon Z8 offers tone modes to control the captured dynamic range (range of brightness levels) in your videos.

But this option isn't available for all video formats. Here's a breakdown:

When to Choose a Tone Mode:

Tone mode selection applies to these video formats:

- N-RAW 12-bit (NEV)
- ProRes RAW HQ 12-bit (MOV)
- ProRes 422 HQ 10-bit (MOV)
- H.265 10-bit (MOV)

Available Tone Modes:

- **SDR (Standard Dynamic Range):** This mode captures a normal range of brightness levels, suitable for most everyday shooting situations. It's compatible with all the above video formats.

- **HLG (Hybrid Log Gamma):** This mode captures a wider dynamic range than SDR, offering more detail in highlights and shadows. However, HLG is only compatible with the H.265 10-bit (MOV) format.

- **N-Log:** This mode captures the widest dynamic range, ideal for professional editing. It uses a specific logarithmic curve that requires color correction in post-production using 3D LUTs (Look Up Tables). N-Log is compatible with the N-RAW, ProRes RAW HQ, and ProRes 422 HQ formats.

Choosing the Right Tone Mode:

- **For everyday use and easy editing:** Choose SDR for a natural look.

- **For capturing a wider dynamic range with some post-processing flexibility:** Choose HLG (compatible only with H.265 10-bit).

- **For maximum dynamic range and professional color grading:** Choose N-Log (compatible with N-RAW, ProRes RAW HQ, and ProRes 422 HQ).

Note: Videos recorded in H.265 8-bit (MOV) and H.264 8-bit (MP4) formats do not offer tone mode selection. They are locked to the SDR range.

ISO Settings for Movie Recording

A part of getting the right exposure for your movies is the ISO sensitivity setting. Effective adjustment of it in the Nikon Z8 may be done as follows:

Maximum Sensitivity: This option establishes the maximum ISO the camera may automatically utilize in different shooting modes:

- **Program (P) Mode:** The shutter speed and aperture are chosen by the camera automatically.
- **Aperture Priority (S) Mode:** The shutter speed is adjusted by the camera while you select the aperture.
- **Shutter Priority (A) Mode:** The camera manipulates the aperture as you pick the shutter speed.
- **Manual (M) Mode (with Auto ISO control ON):** The camera automatically adjusts ISO within the maximum range you choose for shutter speed and aperture.

Note: Select, from ISO 200 to Hi 2.0, the highest ISO setting you can use comfortably. Though it enables filming in low light, higher ISO also adds undesired noise (grain) that may lower the quality of the video.

Manual (M) Mode Automatic ISO Adjustments are also managed and determined by this Setting:

ON: Using your selected shutter speed and aperture in Manual mode, the camera will automatically adjust ISO to maintain appropriate exposure.

OFF: The camera will maintain ISO at the amount you manually enter in M mode, independent of illumination. Should the illumination change, this might produce films that are either overexposed (too bright) or underexposed (too dark).

ISO Sensitivity (Mode M): This option enables you to manually choose the ISO value for video recording in Manual (M) mode; the range is ISO 64 (lowest noise) to Hi 2.0 (brightest but most noise).

Furthermore, constantly balancing exposure and noise, high ISO settings let you take more pictures in low light but also increase noise.

Low ISO settings: May need stronger illumination or shorter shutter speeds (which might result in blur) but produce cleaner, quieter recordings.

Finding the Appropriate Spot: Play around with various ISO settings to get the ideal brightness and acceptable noise levels for your video recordings. Recall that you can usually somewhat modify noise levels in post-processing.

Notes on Reducing Noise with Higher ISO:

- Shoot in proper light settings.
- If you want to shoot videos continually (several videos in a period), think about using a tripod, which will let you shoot at slower shutter speeds and maybe with lower ISO.
- To prevent automatic ISO from exceeding limits and adding too much noise, choose a lower "Maximum Sensitivity" setting.

Chapter Ten

Addressing Common Z8 Troubleshooting Issues

The Nikon Z8 has a range of impressive features, but even the most advanced cameras can experience occasional issues. Here are solutions to resolving 15 common issues that Nikon Z8 users may encounter:

Battery Drains Rapidly

Here are some solutions, if your battery doesn't last:

- Make sure to turn off Bluetooth and Wi-Fi when they are not being used. Enable the Auto Power Off feature to conveniently have the camera turn off automatically when it's not being used for a while.
- Choose authentic Nikon batteries and avoid extreme temperatures.

Blurry Images

If your images always come out with low quality or are not clear, this is what to do:

- Make sure to carefully attach the lens and ensure that autofocus (AF) is enabled.
- For optimal stability in low light conditions, it is recommended to use a tripod.
- Additionally, to effectively capture faster-moving subjects, adjusting the shutter speed is important.

Blackouts During Viewfinder Use

This is what to do when you experience a blackout:

- It is important to regularly update the camera firmware to address this issue.

- Ensure the lens connections are clean and make necessary adjustments to the viewfinder diopter for a clear view.

Autofocus Not Working Properly

This is what to do when the autofocus doesn't function appropriately:

- Ensure that you select the correct AF mode based on your subject.
- Use the single-point AF mode for stationary subjects and the continuous AF mode for moving subjects.
- Make sure to have proper lighting and keep the front and rear elements of your lens clean.

Unable to Record Videos

To solve the issue of your camera being unable to be used for shooting movies, this is what to do:

- Ensure that there is enough space on your memory card and use a high-speed UHS Speed Class 3 (V30) or faster card.
- To optimize performance, it is recommended to format the memory card directly in the camera.

Image Noise

Images may appear grainy due to high noise, however, to address this issue, see what to do:

- It is recommended to reduce the ISO sensitivity, especially in bright environments.
- Navigate to the noise reduction settings in the camera menu.
- Consider shooting in RAW format to enhance your control over noise reduction in post-processing software.

The Camera is Slow in Performance

Sometimes your camera may become slow when you are using it. If you notice this, follow the steps below:

- Make sure you have the most up-to-date firmware installed. Consider updating the firmware of your memory card if it is available.
- It's always a good idea to consult the manufacturer for guidance. It would be helpful to close any unnecessary background applications and format the memory card.

Camera Overheating

Overheating is often caused when you use the camera non-stop for extended periods:

- To prevent your camera from overheating, it is recommended to avoid recording videos for extended periods in hot environments.
- Please turn off the camera and allow it to cool down before continuing to use it.
- Consider using external cooling solutions specifically designed for cameras, which can be purchased from third-party vendors.

Images Not Transferring to Computer

This is what to do:

- Ensure a secure connection between the camera and computer using the appropriate cable.
- Make sure the camera is set to playback mode and try connecting it to a different USB port on your computer.

Downloaded Images Appear Corrupted

This is what to do if you experience this:

- Reformatting the memory card in the camera can help resolve this issue.
- Consider trying a different card reader on your computer.
- Or try using data recovery software to recover corrupted images. It's important to exercise caution and choose reputable software providers.

Trouble getting your camera to focus on close-up subjects

This is what to do when you cannot capture micro images:

- Simply switch to the camera's macro mode, or use a lens specifically designed for macro photography. This will help you capture those up-close shots with ease.
- Also, make sure you are positioned at the appropriate distance from your lens.

Distorted Images

This is what to do:

- To minimize lens flare and prevent image distortion, consider using a lens hood.
- Make sure the lens is securely attached and in good condition.
- Ensure that you review the settings that could potentially lead to distortion, such as the digital zoom feature.

Accidental Setting Changes

Below are quick fixes:

- It's important to become familiar with the camera's menu system and button functions.

- Make sure to use the camera's lock function to avoid any unintended changes to settings, especially in important shooting scenarios.

Trouble with the touchscreen features

In any event that you cannot use the camera touchscreen gestures, do the following:

- Just make sure to keep the touchscreen clean and free of any moisture or debris. That should do the trick.
- Make the necessary adjustments to the touch screen sensitivity settings in the camera menu.
- However, if the touchscreen problem persists, you might want to try using the physical buttons instead, until you get it fixed.

Conclusion

In conclusion, the Nikon Z8 is an extraordinary camera that offers a wealth of features and capabilities to both novice and experienced photographers. Throughout this book, we've embarked on a comprehensive journey, beginning with the fundamental aspects of getting started with your camera, to mastering its advanced functionalities and troubleshooting common issues.

Starting with Chapter One, we introduced the Nikon Z8, highlighting its significance and potential. Chapter Two guided you through the initial setup, ensuring that you are well-versed in configuring the essential settings such as language selection, time zone, and date. We also covered the critical aspects of battery installation, lens attachment, and memory card installation, providing a solid foundation for using your Z8.

In Chapter Three, we delved into the camera's external buttons and controls, offering a detailed overview of the top, back, and front view controls. This chapter aimed to familiarize you with the camera's physical interface, making it easier to navigate and utilize its features effectively.

Chapter Four focused on the various metering modes, providing insights into selecting the right metering method for different shooting scenarios. We explored matrix metering, center-weighted metering, spot metering, and highlight-weighted metering, as well as managing noise in metering to enhance your photographic outcomes.

The power of HDR and bracketing features were thoroughly examined in Chapters Five and Six. Understanding and utilizing these functions can significantly improve your image quality, allowing for greater dynamic range and better exposure in challenging lighting conditions.

In Chapter Seven, we addressed the flash functionalities of the Z8. From electronic flash to high-speed sync, and external flash usage, this chapter provided a comprehensive guide to mastering flash photography with your Z8.

Chapter Eight covered the various exposure modes, including aperture priority, shutter priority, program mode, and manual mode. Mastering these modes, along with understanding f-stops, shutter speeds, and ISO settings, is crucial for achieving the desired exposure and creative effects in your photographs.

Chapter Nine was dedicated to movie shooting, detailing the basic operation, video file types, tone modes, and ISO settings specific to movie recording. This chapter aims to equip you with the knowledge needed to create high-quality videos with your Z8.

Finally, Chapter Ten addressed common troubleshooting issues, offering solutions to problems such as rapid battery drain, autofocus issues, and image noise. This chapter serves as a valuable resource for resolving potential challenges you may encounter while using your Z8.

Therefore, from the above, the Nikon Z8 is a versatile and powerful tool that, when mastered, can elevate your photography and videography to new heights. This book has provided you with the essential knowledge and practical tips to harness the full potential of your camera.

www.ingramcontent.com/pod-product-compliance
Lightning Source LLC
Chambersburg PA
CBHW050232230526
45470CB00005B/1918